ROME
EMPIRE WITHOUT END

by **G. B. Cobbold**

Classics Department, Tabor Academy, Marion, Massachusetts

am

 Wayside®
PUBLISHING
waysidepublishing.com
(888) 302-2519

hello

Other photo and text credits appear on pages where they appear.

(All translations by the author unless otherwise stated.)

Print Date: 1103

ISBN 1-877653-86-1

Table of Contents:

Maps:

Tables/Charts:

PART I
SPQR

1. The Founding Fathers

Aeneas and the Fall of Troy

The story begins at Troy.

For ten years, the Greeks have been attacking the city without success. A blockade has not worked, nor frontal assault. Hector, the Trojans' best fighter, has been killed in single combat with Achilles, but the Trojan army will not surrender, and Troy still stands. The Greeks are exhausted.

Only a trick, perhaps, can bring the city down. And so Odysseus (or Ulysses, as the Romans called him) suggests the clever deception of the wooden horse. This is a huge hollow creature made of maple which is abandoned on the beach outside the city walls while the Greeks ostentatiously put out to sea. The Trojans are perplexed. Where have the Greeks gone? Why have they left the horse behind them? And what is it for? Is it some kind of offering to the Trojan gods? Some want to bring it inside the city, but Laocoon, Neptune's high priest in Troy, is highly suspicious. In a poem written many generations later, we can still hear his protests, and learn what happened next:

> *"Don't you understand that anything that a Greek brings to you is a trick of some sort? ... There's certainly something wrong. Don't trust this horse. Whatever it is, I'm afraid of the Greeks – especially when they come with gifts"...*
>
> *At that very moment... a pair of serpents come*

Greek vase-painting: Aeneas escaping from Troy with his father on his back, and with his wife Creusa following him. (Photograph © 2004 Museum of Fine Arts, Boston)

swimming in to the beach, side by side, necks held up straight, eyes glaring. The blood-colored crests on their heads show up above the surface, the water swirling and curling down the length of their backs in trails of spray. They reach the land. Their hot eyes are swollen with fire and blood, and their flickering tongues hiss wet in their mouths... still they come on, and head for the altar, where Laocoon the priest, who is sacrificing, according to proper ritual, a great bull. First the snakes wind themselves around the bodies of his two children, opening their jaws wide over their poor little arms and legs. As he comes rushing to help them, his knife in his hand, they seize him too, coiling and coiling about him. They twist twice around his waist, and twice around his neck; they rear their scaly backs above his head while he tries to untangle their knotted bodies.

(Vergil: *Aeneid* ii 40, 202)

The message is clear. No one should listen to any advice that does not welcome the horse; anyone who gives such advice is doomed. And so the Trojans dismantle their gates so that the horse can be dragged inside the city, and they spend the night in celebration. By the small hours of the morning, after much singing and dancing and drinking, they are all asleep.

And now a party of Greek soldiers, who have all this time been hidden in the horse's belly, lower themselves down onto the ground. They flash a signal, and the Greek fleet, which after all has only hidden itself behind an island, silently returns. Their troops disembark, and through the broken gates they enter the city.

The Trojans, still half-asleep, offer no resistance. The city is sacked; its women and children are sold into slavery. Only a handful escape: among them is the warrior Aeneas, who with his wife, his son, his father and a few companions, makes his way through the burning streets to safety in the nearby mountains. There he is encouraged by the gods to make his way westwards to found a

new city at a spot where he will find a huge white sow with thir-
ty piglets sucking at her teats.

Obediently Aeneas sets out on his journey. He has many
adventures on the high seas and in foreign lands: he visits Sicily
and is chased away by the same Cyclopes who had threatened
Odysseus; he crosses the river Styx to the underworld; he is
wrecked in north Africa and delayed there by the blandishments
of Dido, queen of Carthage (a city one day to be famous in Roman
history). But the gods will not let him linger there, and he departs
unwillingly for his final stopping place in western Italy, where on
the banks of the river Tiber he comes upon the white sow and her
litter at last.

The region is called Latium, its people and its language Latin.
The local chieftain welcomes Aeneas, and offers him the hand of
his daughter Lavinia in marriage. After a brief war against forces
led by Lavinia's former fiancé, Aeneas marries her and then,
according to his divine destiny, he founds his city. Later his son
Ascanius founds another city, Alba Longa, which is ruled there-
after by a dynasty of distinguished kings.

Romulus and Remus

One day, there was a crisis in Alba Longa. The rightful king
had been driven out of the city by his wicked brother, and the
king's daughter, Rhea Silvia, was locked up so that she might not
bear any children who might become legitimate heirs to the
throne. Nevertheless, she became mysteriously and scandalously
pregnant by Mars, the god of war, and gave birth to twin sons,
Romulus and Remus. The usurper decided that he must get rid of
them, and yet their deaths must not appear to be his fault. So he
placed them in a wooden box, and set it afloat down the river
Tiber, which was at that moment in flood. When the flood reced-
ed, the box was left unexpectedly high and dry, and the twins were
rescued by a wolf, which reared them until a shepherd took them
away to his house.

As the twins grew up, their qualities of leadership became so

Bronze statue: Romulus and Remus nursed by the wolf. The figure of the wolf is Etruscan, but the twins were added later. (Art Resource)

noticeable to all their friends that it became clear that they must be of royal blood. At the head of a gang of local teenagers, they led a rebellion against the usurper, assassinated him and restored the original king to the throne of Alba Longa. But this first taste of power did not satisfy them; and they resolved to found a city of their own, which they established at a bend in the river on seven low-lying hills.

The construction of the city was soon completed, except for its defensive walls. At this point an acrimonious discussion broke out between the brothers about which of them the city should be named after. To settle their argument they sought the advice of the gods, which they believed would be revealed to them by the behavior of vultures flying high in the sky. But when the vultures eventually appeared, the brothers argued bitterly about how to interpret the meaning of their flight. In the end, Remus taunted Romulus by jumping over his half of the unfinished wall. Romulus then picked up a rake and killed his brother. So the city was called Rome, and this the moment from which the Romans would calculate all subsequent dates in their history. In the modern system of recording historical events, the date was 753 BC.

The new city of Rome was filled at first by fugitives, refugees and outcasts—anyone who wanted to make a fresh start under a new regime. Romulus governed them fairly with the advice of a group of a hundred older men, the fathers of the first hundred families he had accepted into his settlement. The group was called the Senate—or the *patres conscripti*—and from then on it functioned, with modifications, as the central institution of the Roman government. Under this system, all went well until Romulus' sudden realization that there were not enough women among his subjects to guarantee the growth of the population. He therefore decided to stage a festival to celebrate the anniversary of Rome's foundation, and he invited the people of a nearby tribe, the Sabines, to attend. When everyone was absorbed in the festival, Romulus gave a signal, and each Roman man seized a young Sabine woman. The Sabine men were apparently hurried away without significant protest, and so the problem of the population was solved.

Romulus reigned for forty years—and then he disappeared. The legend suggests that he did not die, but rather was snatched up into the sky like the prophet Elijah in the Old Testament.

> *One day when Romulus was inspecting his army... there was suddenly a violent thunderstorm and he was completely hidden from sight by a thick cloud, and from that time on he was never seen again.*
>
> *The soldiers, who had been alarmed by the storm, recovered their nerve when the sun reappeared, but Romulus' throne was empty. The soldiers believed the senators, who had been standing by him, when they said that he had been carried up by a whirlwind. But nevertheless they felt like children who had lost their father, and they stood for a long time in sad silence. Then some people began to claim that Romulus had gone to heaven, and in the end everyone agreed that since he was the son*

*of a god he was a god himself, and they prayed that he
would forever be kind to them and protect them...*

    *A man called Proculus later addressed the assembly,
and he told the people that Romulus had left him the following message: "By the wish of the gods, my city will
be the capital of the world. Let my people learn to be
fighters. And let them be assured, and let their children
be assured, that there is no earthly power than can ever
resist the Romans."*

                                   (Livy: *History* i.16)

    That, at any rate, was the story. Was it true? The later Romans certainly enjoyed believing most of what they were told about Aeneas and Romulus, but they did not accept all of it as fact. For example, most of them viewed the story of the Sabine women as a myth. Nor did they take very seriously the tale of the twins' rescue by the wolf: this was in fact probably invented to give Romulus the same kind of legendary respectability as figures like Oedipus, king of Thebes, or Cyrus the Great of Persia, who were also said to have been abandoned as infants and brought up by animals or shepherds. (At the other end of the Mediterranean, the Hebrews told a similar story about their heroic forebear Moses, who had been floated down the Nile and rescued by an Egyptian princess.) All we know for certain from the archaeological evidence is that Rome began as a small village in Latium, and only very gradually became larger and more important than its neighbors.

Latins and Etruscans

    The earliest inhabitants of Italy were farmers, who led harsh and demanding lives on poor soil which was irrigated with difficulty from the available water. They survived hardship by demonstrating characteristics that the Romans would always value in themselves—tenacity, seriousness of purpose, and the ability to put up with the worst in order to achieve the best.

The inhabitants of Latium probably arrived as part of the major migrations into Italy that took place about 1000 BC. Perhaps they were of the same stock as the Dorians, who at about the same time had made their way into Greece and occupied the ruins of the Mycenaean citadels. The Latins settled in the west-central part of Italy, whenever possible on hilltops, as a defense against their enemies. The site of Rome—pigs and oak-trees aside—was an especially advantageous one because it lay at a ford of the Tiber and thus could control the north-south route which crossed the river as well as boat traffic up and down it. The Tiber turned out to be one of the few navigable rivers of Italy, and because its mouth at Ostia was not regularly silted up, it could be developed as a port.

At roughly the same time as the Latins were settling in Latium, another people, the Etruscans, who may have come originally from Asia, were establishing themselves just to the north, in the area which they called Etruria (modern Tuscany). They were highly inventive and artistic, and became very prosperous. They used iron weapons, sailed fast ships and drove chariots. They had a system of writing that used a version of the Greek alphabet and so can more or less be sounded out—although their language has not yet been deciphered.

There is archaeological evidence that the less sophisticated Romans soon came under the cultural influence of the Etruscans, and were at least occasionally dominated by them politically as well. Most of the architecture of early Rome had Etruscan features—bridges, arches, and the main drain (which still exists) called the *Cloaca Maxima*. The Romans also took from Etruria the long draped mantle called the *toga*, which Roman men always wore on formal occasions. Every Roman magistrate was always escorted by *lictors*, who carried another Etruscan borrowing, the *fasces*—a ceremonial bundle of sticks with an axe protruding from it which represented the magistrate's power to inflict corporal or capital punishment. Many of the Etruscan gods became the gods of Rome, and retained their Etruscan names even after they became identified with the Olympian gods of Greece. And Roman priests also imitated the Etruscan practice of seeking the will of the gods by augury—that is, by reading omens in thunder and lightning, in the behavior of birds, or in the arrangement of the internal organs of sacrificed animals.

The Tarquins and Lucretia

After Romulus, legend begins to turn slowly but firmly into history: a series of seven kings appear to have ruled for two hundred and fifty years with varying degrees of benevolence. Under the first four kings, there were long periods of peace during which Roman influence spread down the Tiber to Ostia, and the religious calendar was organized; and also outbreaks of war with Rome's neighbors, particularly Alba Longa, which was finally removed as a possible rival. As a result of a some kind of alliance with the Etruscans, or of Roman women marrying into the Etruscan royal family, the next kings came from Etruria: Tarquinius Priscus, Servus Tullius and Tarquinius Superbus (Tarquin the Proud).

Tarquin the Proud was the last king of Rome. Unlike any of his predecessors, he was hated for his harsh edicts, his arbitrary cruelty and in particular for the excesses of his son Sextus, Tarquinius. Sextus is supposed to have raped a woman called Lucretia, while her husband Collatinus was away at war. Lucretia, in mortification, stabbed herself to death, leaving Collatinus a vengeful widower. Encouraged by two companions, he swore an oath to expel the king, and in 509 BC he raised a bloody revolution in the streets of the city. Tarquin and his family fled north, to the Etruscan capital of Clusium.

The Romans then promised themselves that never again would they be ruled by a king, and, in place of the monarchy, a republic was established. The city would now be governed by magistrates who were to be elected annually by all the citizens— or rather by all male citizens over the age of eighteen. The two chief administrative officers were called *consuls*; and the first consuls were Collatinus himself and Lucius Junius Brutus, who ever afterwards was revered as the founder of the Roman republic.

2. The Roman People and the Roman Constitution

Families

organized

By the time that Rome had become a republic, the city had grown into a more or less organized conglomeration of houses, temples, law courts, workshops and markets, all arranged about a central square, called in Latin the *forum*, and linked by roads and bridges to the agricultural countryside which surrounded it. A diversity of occupations inevitably divided its inhabitants into groups based on social class or wealth. There were slaves—prisoners of war or their descendants—and there were citizens—rich landowners and small farmers; all manner of craftsmen; bankers, moneylenders and shopkeepers; priests; artists and musicians. And there were the citizens' wives and daughters—seen and not heard, just as they had been in most of the cities of ancient Greece.

For inhabitants of any rank the basic unit of Roman society was the family, and a Roman man's names were often a potted version of his family history. Roman men had at least two names: a personal name (*praenomen*) and a family name (*nomen*). Often a third name (*cognomen*) was added, which either described connections by marriage to other families or some special achievement or physical characteristic of an ancestor; examples of *cognomina* are Magnus (the Great), Naso (Long Nosed) or Caesar (Hairy).

The family consisted of everyone in a household, including slaves, ruled by the head of the family, the *paterfamilias*. In Roman law, he had the right to put to death his children or his slaves for any act of disobedience or disloyalty. He was responsible for the welfare of all his family members, especially for the education of his children. For several centuries education took placed entirely within the home (the first school was not established until about 200), and at first the curriculum was very simple. Little Latin literature existed, and reading and writing were of limited use even to the rich and powerful. But children could certainly be taught good behavior, and particularly to defer to their elders and betters, to pay attention to the legends of heroes of the past, and to revere the gods—all according to the *mos maiorum,* or ancestral custom.

As important as ancestral custom were the ancestors themselves; not only were they regarded seriously as worthy examples of behavior, but they were also actually worshiped. Portrait busts of famous forebears were prominently displayed in private houses, and their ashes were kept in a shrine, along with the images of the household gods—the *Lares* and the *Penates*.

Society

Roman families were divided into two groups or social orders: a comparatively small number of aristocratic *patricians,* the descendants of Romulus' first hundred senators, who had become rich because they had early gained control of the best land, and everyone else, the *plebeians* or *plebs*, who were the small farmers, the tradesman, craftsmen and unskilled workers. All male citizens, patrician or plebeian, had the vote, but in other respects the two orders had separate social and political rights; and for more than two centuries, the plebeians campaigned to gain equality with the patricians.

The eventual fusing of the two orders, so that all distinctions between them disappeared, was a demonstration of the Romans' skill in changing their institutions without destroying their traditions. In the first two hundred and fifty years of the republic's history there were few violent upheavals, and little drama. There were no radical reformers like Lycurgus in Sparta, or Solon or Cleisthenes in Athens; there was no more than sporadic scuffling in the streets. Rather Roman society evolved unspectacularly over many generations like a bioorganism, changing only as it needed to change. Though the Romans loved to argue and protest, changes in Roman life seem to have been part of an almost inevitable process, brought about as much by the patricians' real-

Man of the Republic. (Photograph © 2004 Museum of Fine Arts, Boston)

ization that the time to share their power had come as by any unrelenting determination or revolutionary spirit on the part of the plebeians.

The significant events of what is usually called "the struggle of the orders" were for the most part unspectacular, except for the occasion in 494 when the plebs went on strike, downed tools and gathered on a hillside outside the city; they dispersed only when certain concessions were made to them. In 450, the Senate had posted in the forum for everyone to see the so-called Twelve Tables—a list of laws, never before published, primarily involving contracts, inheritances, the emancipation of slaves and the rights of women. Like the laws of Hammurabi in Mesopotamia or Draco in Athens, their publication prevented any magistrate from making arbitrary interpretations of the law to suit his own purposes. Five years later the *lex Canuleia* introduced an important amendment to the Twelve Tables which allowed patricians and plebeians to intermarry, and in 326 it became illegal to force anyone into slavery because of inability to pay off his debts.

Magistrates

After the expulsion of the kings in 509, the functions and powers of the kings were divided among annually elected magistrates. The most important of them were the *consuls*. There were two of them, each with the right to forbid any action of the other, so that their powers were properly checked and balanced. They were the heads of state, invested by the Senate with *imperium*— the authority to oversee domestic and judicial affairs and to lead armies in war. As with all the magistracies, their *imperium* was clearly defined, and the terms of their service were strictly limited, in order to remove the possibility that one man could ever again make himself a king: for instance, a ten-year interval had to elapse before anyone could be re-elected to any office. And as with all the magistracies, the consulship was originally only open to patricians, but was later opened to the plebs.

As the state's business became more complex, other magistrates became necessary. *Praetors*, originally the consuls' deputies, were responsible for the operation of the lawcourts and the interpretation of the law. *Quaestors* looked after financial affairs. Two *censors* made certain that the voters' lists were up to date, in order to prevent corruption at the polls, and they had the prestigious task of appointing members of the senate and striking off the rolls any members whose morality came into question; they were also in charge of public works. The most famous censor was Appius Claudius, who in 312 constructed Rome's first aqueduct and the famous road—the *Via Appia*, or Appian Way—which ran north-south along most of the length of the Italian peninsula and later helped the Romans to spread their influence and culture throughout the whole of Italy.

In response to the plebeians' strike of 494, a special magistracy was created. Ten *tribunes* were elected solely by the plebs, and were committed to looking out specifically for plebeian interests. Since the tribunes had the support of the great majority of the people, they had considerable power; and even their persons were constitutionally protected—that is, it was illegal, under pain of death, to harm them in any way, or even to jostle them in the street. More importantly, they could propose legislation and could veto the act of any other magistrate, or even the senate, if they did not think that the plebeian cause was being served.

The tribunes' assistants were the *aediles*, who eventually achieved responsibilities of their own: they kept a check on the accuracy of weights and measures, and were supposed to make sure that the streets and public buildings were kept clean. They were also the producers of the games and gladiatorial shows that were often used to soothe popular discontent. They would organize games that were as lavish and fantastic as possible, even if it meant going into debt, in the hope that they would be rewarded with votes when they ran for higher office.

All Roman magistrates—including the chief priest, the *pontifex maximus*—were elected annually, and they all served without pay. Thus only the rich could afford to stand for election. Since the city's wealth at this point was mainly in the hands of the patricians, this meant that for the most part only patricians were elected, even though the offices were legally open to everyone. Standing for office frequently became a family tradition, and equally it became a tradition to vote for members of the same family—so that, for example, between 234 and 134 nearly 80 percent of the consuls came from the same twenty-six families. Those who could claim a consul as an ancestor were known as *nobiles* (nobles), and anyone running for consul for the first time in his family's history was disparagingly known as a *novus homo* (new man). In fact the magistrates were an aristocratic oligarchy, with a common conservative point of view; and electoral contests were frequently less a matter of political differences but rather a private squabble between two members of noble families.

The Senate and People of Rome

The *Senate*, the council of elders founded by Romulus, was not disbanded with the end of the monarchy. During the first years of the republic's existence Romulus' original hundred members grew to three hundred, and were increased much later to six hundred. New senators, originally nominated by the king, were appointed in the early republic by the consuls or the censors; but in 80 all ex-magistrates automatically became senators, which meant that the whole Senate was eventually indirectly elected by the people. Membership in the Senate was for life, and therefore the senators, easily identified by the broad purple stripe that they wore along the edges of their togas, had long experience and great prestige. To maintain their elite status and to separate them from the rest of the people, they were not allowed to involve themselves in trade, nor could they leave Italy without the permission of their colleagues.

Only in certain matters of finance and foreign affairs (including the ratification of treaties) did the Senate have specific legal capacity. Its real power lay in the advice that it would give not only to the magistrates but also, crucially, to the people. In the various popular assemblies, the citizens—plebeians and patricians alike—would discuss and vote upon proposals to change the laws or introduce new ones, to hear appeals against the judicial decisions of the consuls and praetors, or to declare war. But according to long tradition, the assemblies would not come to any decision unless they were guided and advised by the Senate. As a result, the Senate's opinions (*senatus consulta*) came to be considered as valid as law, and the joint authority of the Senate and the people was signified by the letters SPQR *(Senatus Populusque Romanus)* that appeared in public places and on public documents.

But the Romans in fact were not particularly interested in day-to-day politics. As the number of citizens increased, and as more and more of them lived further and further away from the city itself, fewer of them tended to show up for meetings of the assemblies. They were content to elect aristocratic nobles to public office, and to leave the real decisions to the Senate, so that the *senatus consulta* came to substitute for democratic action. Roman citizens rarely felt the political passion of the fifth century Athenians, and Roman democracy was always more theoretical than real.

With their accustomed seriousness. Roman senators gather in their togas on the steps of a temple. (Art Resource)

3. Roman Expansion in Italy

Rome and the Etruscans

During the two centuries that the "Struggle of the Orders" was working out the machinery of the Roman constitution, the Romans' activity was not confined to domestic affairs. The system that they established turned out to serve them well during a long period of expansion, consisting both of military campaigns and diplomatic maneuvers, as the insignificant city-state in Latium slowly gained control over the whole of Italy.

After the expulsion of the kings in 509, Rome was at once invaded by the Etruscans under their king Lars Porsenna, who was determined to restore the Tarquin family to their throne. The invasion was repulsed, but it marked the beginning of more than a hundred years of war between the two states, at the end of which the Romans overcame Etruscan resistance and absorbed Etruria into their own territory. It is a period of half-history and half-legend from which emerged many of the famous stories about the

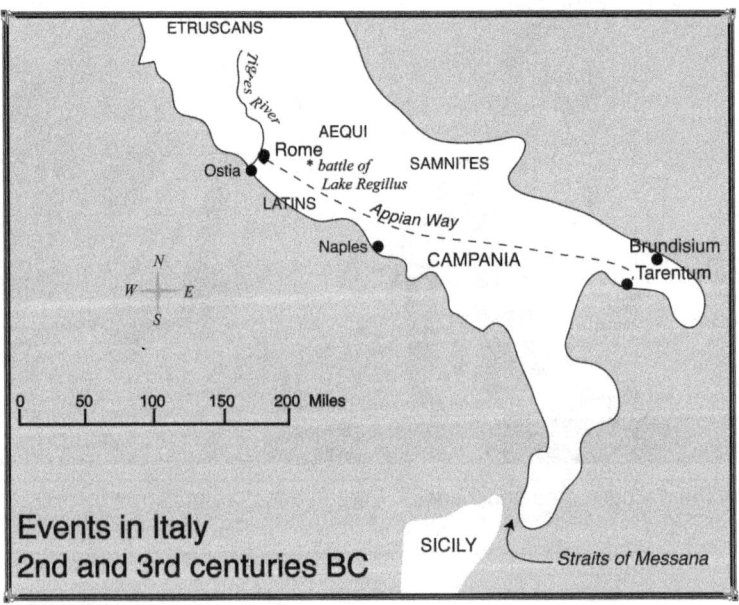

Events in Italy
2nd and 3rd centuries BC

gallantry and determination of their forebears which the Romans proudly repeated to their children, whether they were really true or not.

They remembered, for instance, how Horatius singlehandedly held the last bridge across the Tiber against an Etruscan army of overwhelming strength. They remembered how Quintus Mucius, who had set out to assassinate Lars Porsenna in his camp, stabbed the king's secretary by mistake; and how, when captured by the Etruscans, Mucius held his right hand over an open flame, refusing to disclose information about the Roman strategy and promising that all Roman soldiers could stand pain as well as he; and how Lars Porsenna, overcome with awe and apprehension, decided to release Mucius and sue for peace, while Mucius himself was given the *cognomen* of Scaevola (the left-handed). And they remembered how the important Etruscan stronghold of Veii fell in 396 to a general with the resounding name of Marcus Furius Camillus, who was said to have driven a tunnel under its walls and to have emerged with his troops in the middle of the astonished enemy.

Rome, Latins and Italians

As the war with the Etruscans proceeded, the Romans also were involved in campaigns against the neighboring Latin towns, and the Italian tribes to the south. As the Romans developed the fighting skills of their army, with its phalanx-like legions of infantrymen, armed with short jabbing swords and javelins, progress was slow and unspectacular, but thorough. As early as 496, they fought a decisive battle with the Latins at Lake Regillus, where the twin gods Castor and Pollux were supposed to have intervened on behalf of the Romans. But the most interesting consequence of the battle was a constitutional amendment, whereby for the first time the Senate appointed a new kind of magistrate. In a crisis (usually a military crisis), special *imperium* would be given to a *dictator*, whose authority would override that of all other magistrates or commanders. However there was a special proviso: on the theory that if he could deal with the crisis at all, he could deal with it quickly, a dictator was appointed only for a six-month period. It was considered that a longer period of supreme power would be not only dangerous to the system of checks and balances of power so carefully built into the constitution, but might even lead to what the Romans always feared the most, the restoration of the monarchy.

The Roman historian Livy, writing of a defeat by the Aequi, a tribe of central Italy, remarks the Roman suspicion of one particular dictator, even though he seemed completely without pretension:

> *The city was in confusion, and the people were just as terrified as if Rome itself were under siege… It was a moment for the Senate to appoint a dictator, and without objection Lucius Quinctius Cincinnatus was named. Now those people who think that money is all-important, and that only rich men can become powerful and successful, should look at the case of Cincinnatus. The only man who the Romans thought could save them was at that moment working on his small farm… The messengers from Rome found him hard at work preparing the ground for planting. "May the gods bless you and our country," they said. "Put on your toga, and listen to the orders of the Senate."*
>
> *Cincinnatus was taken back. He asked if all were well, and asked his wife to fetch his toga from the house. When it arrived, he wiped the mud off his face before he put it on. The messengers then congratulated him on his appointment as dictator. They explained the military situation and required him to come to Rome; a ship, they said, was waiting to carry him down the Tiber… In Rome he was welcomed by his sons, relatives and friends, and by most of the senators assembled. Surrounded by this crowd, and escorted by lictors, he proceeded to his town house. The ordinary people, however, were less delight-*

ed; they were anxious about the dictator's power and how he might use it.

(Livy: *History* iii.26)

Eventually the resistance of the Latins and Italians collapsed, and each town was linked to Rome by a special treaty or alliance. Together they formed a confederacy of allied states with Rome at its head; they paid no tribute, and their only obligation was to supply troops to the Roman army. In return the Romans came to expect their loyalty, and on only a very few future occasions did they not receive it.

Rome and the Gauls ⚔

Meanwhile there were enemies from further afield who also had to be faced. At the end of the fifth century, Celtic tribes called Gauls, exotic with their long wild hair and their shrill war-cries, had wandered across the Alps and settled in northwest Italy. In 390, the most restless and belligerent of these Gauls came swooping south, plundering their way through the territory of Rome's new allies, and were finally met by the Roman army only ten miles from the city, on the bank of the river Allia. Greatly outnumbered, the Romans were severely defeated, and the Gauls entered Rome.

The facts of this humiliation were later modified in the usual way, in order to discover within them examples of Roman virtue. As the Romans remembered the story, the Gauls wandered into the city like awestruck tourists, their eyes bulging at what, by their standards, was the magnificence of the unpaved streets and mud-brick houses and thatched temples. When they arrived at the Senate House, they found the senators waiting for them in their official chairs, dignified and majestic as marble statues. One Gaul overcame his timidity and pulled a senatorial beard. The senator hit the Gaul, hard, with his walking stick—a saving of face which only served to break the tension and to trigger the ransacking of the city.

Only the central fortified hill, the Capitol, still held out, in the hands of a garrison led by Manlius. Its steep walls baffled the Gauls for a while, but they finally decided upon a night attack. While the garrison slept, the Gauls crept up the hill; but the sacred geese, which lived on the Capitol in the temple of Juno, raised the alarm. Their cackling woke Manlius just in time for him to turn out the guard—and save the Capitol.

But the Gauls occupied the city for several more months. They finally agreed to withdraw, but only if they were paid a thousand pounds of gold. When the Romans protested that this was too much, the Gauls' leader remarked "*Vae Victis*", which roughly means "Too bad for you—but you're the losers." And as usual, it was the winners who dictated the terms of peace. The Romans reluctantly made the payment, and the Gauls departed, marching all the way back to Gaul—probably because of troubles which needed their attention at home and not, as the Romans liked to think, because they were rolled back by the army of the famous Camillus.

Rome and the Greeks

During the great wave of Greek colonization in the eighth and seventh centuries BC, many Greek towns had been founded in the south of Italy. Southern Italy and Sicily had indeed become so dotted with Greek towns that the region came to be known as Magna Graecia (Great Greece). The Greeks of Italy, like their counterparts on the Greek mainland, had always had difficulty in keeping peace among themselves. About 300, some of the colonists in Magna Graecia, seeing how effectively the Romans had dealt with the Italian tribes, had requested Rome's help in their local squabbles. The squabbles themselves were insignificant, but they became important in 280 when the city of Tarentum called on King Pyrrhus of Epirus (in northwest Greece) for help in what it considered to be Roman interference in their internal affairs.

Epirus was one of the smaller fragments of Alexander the

Great's empire, which had broken up some forty years earlier; and Pyrrhus was descended—so he said—from Alexander himself, and had similar ambitions. He therefore answered the appeal of Tarentum in the hope of achieving a quick conquest of the Greek towns of Italy, and then, perhaps, of persuading some of the Roman allies to come over to his side. Pyrrhus' army was well-disciplined and came complete with elephants imported from India—enormous monsters that at first sight threw the Roman soldiers into a panic. In battle, however, the elephants were used only for the very first charge; after that they became so frightened by the smell of blood that they tended to go berserk and to become equally dangerous to both sides.

Pyrrhus' incursion into Italy ended after a short campaign in which he failed to attain any of his objectives. He did win several pitched battles, but his own losses were too great to tolerate, and none of the Italian allies moved to support his plan for an advance on Rome. In disgust and disappointment at these "Pyrrhic victories", he turned for home, and the Senate wasted no time in incorporating the Greeks of southern Italy into the Roman confederacy.

But this time the Romans gained far more than new allies. They were completely won over by their initial contact with Greek civilization, and religion became the first aspect of Roman culture to be affected. The Romans' traditional beliefs in leprechaun-like nature spirits had been for generations combined with the worship of Etruscan gods and with Etruscan rituals and teachings. Now those Etruscan gods became completely identified with the Greek gods of Mount Olympus; Greek mythology replaced all the tales which had once been told about the Etruscan or Italian gods, and only their Etruscan names (already modified into Latin forms) were left to them.

The Roman Confederacy

By 279 the entire Italian peninsula was included in the Roman confederacy, and Rome had become such a powerful pres-

The Appian Way, with original ancient Roman pavement, bounded by the ubiquitous Italian cypress trees. (Art Resource)

ence in the western Mediterranean that other states had begun to take serious notice of it. The population of the city had grown to nearly a million, of which perhaps three hundred thousand were men of military age; and the strength of the Roman legions was almost doubled by contingents from the towns of the confederacy.

Rome's treatment of her allies seems to have been sensitive and sensible, and they had given their firm support to Rome in the war against Pyrrhus. The confederate towns retained their own governments, but were united by Roman law and order represented by visiting judges, by the spread of Latin as a common language, and by an evolving common culture. People, goods and ideas were transported along the "feathered arrows" of the Appian Way and other Roman roads (so called because they always ran as straight as was practicable and were lined with poplars and cypresses). Moreover, the inhabitants of an increasing number of towns near Rome were made either full citizens or citizens with limited rights. Unlike the Athenian empire of Pericles, the Romans had no need to hold on to their allies' loyalty by force of arms. The Senate, with considerable imagination, understood that economic support and the subsidy of public works programs would be much more effective than garrisons in maintaining harmony within the confederation, and would give it the determination it would need to withstand its next great challenge.

THE MAJOR GREEK AND ROMAN GODS

Greek Name	Roman Name (originally Etruscan)	Function
Zeus	Jupiter	King of gods and mortals
Hera	Juno	Queen of gods and mortals
Aphrodite	Venus	Love
Apollo	Apollo	Sun/ Prophecy/ Poetry
Ares	Mars	War
Artemis	Diana	Moon/ Hunting/ Childbirth/ Chastity
Athene	Minerva	Wisdom/ the Arts
Demeter	Ceres	Agriculture
Hades	Pluto	King of the Underworld
Hephaistos	Vulcan	Fire/ Metalwork
Hermes	Mercury	Messenger of the Gods/ Trade/ Travel/ Trickery
Hestia	Vesta	Hearth/ Home Life
Poseidon	Neptune	Sea/ Water/ Horses

4. The First Punic War: 264 – 241 BC

The Carthaginian Empire

About the time of the end of the Trojan War, according to legend, a princess of Tyre, a Phoenician island-city off the coast of modern Lebanon, had fled to north Africa with a small band of followers, and established there the city of Carthage. She was later identified with queen Dido, who had laid a curse on the future city of Rome after the Trojan fugitive Aeneas had fallen in love with her and then abandoned her.

At the beginning of the third century BC, Carthage was large and prosperous. It was ruled by an oligarchy supported by wealthy merchants and an army of well-paid mercenaries. The Carthaginians were highly competent seamen—a Carthaginian had circumnavigated the African continent while the Romans were building their first bridges across the Tiber—and they had established flourishing colonies in Spain and Sicily, as well as lucrative trade routes outside the Straits of Gibraltar which ran as far north as Britain and down the west coast of Africa. The Carthaginians had long shown an interest in spreading their influence into Italy, and had at one time briefly allied themselves with the Etruscans. As early as 306 they had recognized the growing ascendancy of the Romans, and had signed a treaty with them in which they promised not to encroach on Italy in return for assurances that Rome would not interfere with Carthage's colonies. However a clash between the two states seemed inevitable if Rome were to continue the expansion of its power beyond the coast of Italy.

The Cause of War

The bone of contention between Rome and Carthage turned out to be Sicily, which lies off the toe of Italy across a narrow strait only five miles wide. The city in Sicily nearest to the strait was Messana, a Greek community which in 264, after a complicated quarrel, was occupied by Carthaginian soldiers. The citizens rose in revolt and asked the Romans for their support.

The debate in the Senate on whether or not Messana should be helped was a long and anxious one. If the Carthaginians held on to Messana, they might well use it as a jumping-off point for a future invasion of Italy, and the Romans certainly had a clear obligation to protect their allies, the Greek cities in the south of Italy. The Greeks of Italy, moreover, would not easily tolerate a threat to any of the Greek cities in Sicily with whom they had flourishing trade relations. On the other hand, the Romans did not wish to break the treaty that they had made with Carthage in 306.

In the end, the threat posed by the presence of Carthaginian forces so close to Italy convinced the Romans to take pre-emptive military action. Accordingly they ferried an army across the strait and drove the Carthaginian garrison out of Messana. Messana was at once blockaded by a Carthaginian fleet, at which point the Senate declared war. The hostilities which then began were called by the Romans the Punic War, after the Latin word for "Phoenician."

Campaigns by Land and Sea

The Romans' first aim was to drive the Carthaginians out of Sicily. But to do this their army, no matter how effective, would not be enough: they also would need ships, in order to control the sea-passage between Sicily and Carthage, as well as the strait of Messana.

There were few good natural harbors on the Italian peninsula. Moreover the Romans had no warships and precious few transport vessels, and certainly nothing that would stand up to the Carthaginian navy. As was usual for the Romans, however, necessity became the mother not of invention but of borrowing and modification. They somehow got hold of a Carthaginian warship—their own story was that a Roman farmer stumbled across a wrecked Carthaginian vessel on an Italian beach and reported it to

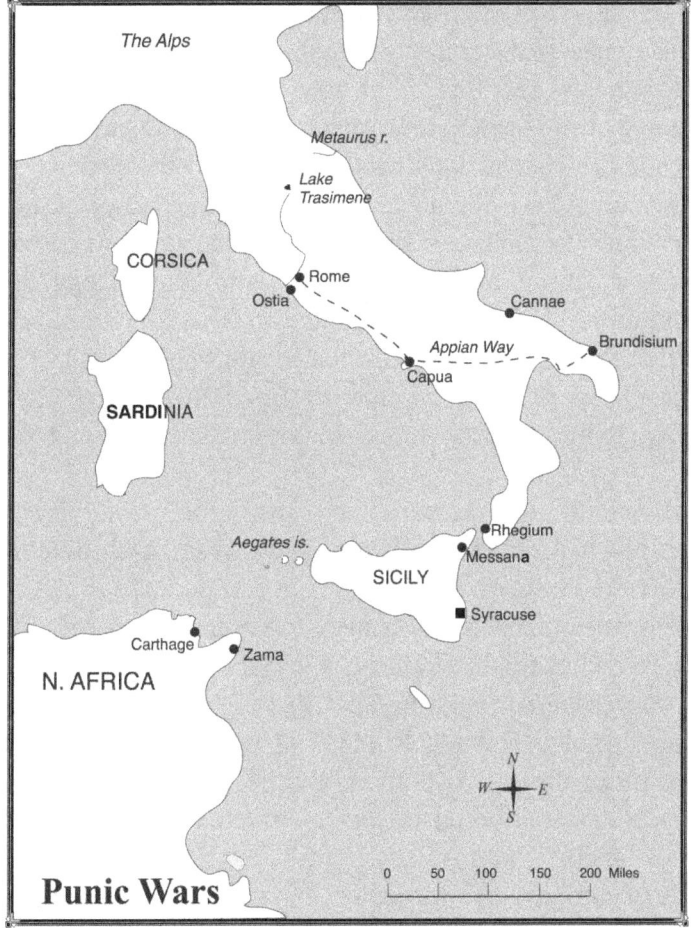

Punic Wars

the Senate, who arranged for the manufacture of a hundred and twenty copies within two months. Then, aware of their own inexperience in seamanship and in particular of their ignorance of naval tactics, the Romans developed a gadget consisting of a wide gangplank, which was kept lashed to the mast in an upright position until a battle was about to begin. The plank could then be lowered onto the deck of an enemy ship and locked into place by an iron spike that resembled a bird's beak and gave the device its name: *corvus* (crow). Roman infantrymen could then cross the gangplank and engage the enemy on his own decks, exactly as they would have done on land.

The new Roman fleet, miraculously constructed, at once achieved equally miraculous success. The *corvus* worked well in its initial trials, and four quick naval victories gave the Romans command of the sea, so that they were able to land their legions first in Sicily (where they captured most of the Sicilian towns), and then in Africa for an attack on Carthage itself. But things turned sour: after a long stalemate, the Carthaginians defeated the Romans in Africa, and captured its commander, Regulus, along with hundreds of his men. Regulus was sent home on parole, on condition that he arrange an exchange of prisoners, but he refused to make any recommendation to the Senate and returned to Carthage to be tortured. He would not break his word, even to the enemy.

Meanwhile the Romans were losing ships, some by storm (the *corvus* made them top-heavy in big seas), and some in a battle which to the superstitious Romans was doomed to failure even before it began. When the Roman commander was informed that the sacred chickens had refused to eat that morning, he had them thrown overboard, declaring angrily, "If they won't eat, they can certainly drink." But the Romans at least were able to replace their sunk or damaged ships, while the Carthaginians ran out of money and were forced to lay up much of their fleet. Off the Aegates Islands, the final battle of the war was fought, after which the Carthaginians sued for peace. They agreed to pay a huge fine to Rome and to evacuate Sicily, which now fell completely under Roman control.

Provinces and Protectorates

So Sicily became the first Roman province, or *provincia*, and new overseas possessions quickly followed. In 225, Sardinia and Corsica were annexed from the Carthaginians, and became the second province. At the same time the Gauls were driven out of northeast Italy; the Romans took their territory under their military protection, called it Cisalpine Gaul (Gaul on this side of the Alps), and built a new road, the Via Flaminia, to link it with the rest of Italy.

Three years later, the Roman fleet went into action in the Adriatic, against the pirates of Illyria (Albania and part of the former Yugoslavia), who had begun to attack Roman merchant ships on passage to the Greek cities of southern Italy. As a result of their victory, the Romans now became involved with mainland Greece: they opened diplomatic relations with Corinth and Athens, who were equally relieved to see the end of the pirates, and began to trade with the Greek cities. Another protectorate was set up in Illyria, in order to guard the sea-route between Italy and Greece, and to protect the entire Adriatic region from the threat of King Philip V of Macedonia.

Almost accidentally, the Romans had established the beginnings of an empire, and had become closely connected with other Mediterranean powers. And they were not yet finished with Carthage.

5. The Second Punic War: 218 – 201 BC

The Outbreak of War

The second Punic war, despite the interval of more than twenty years, was in effect a continuation of the first. The Carthaginians felt oppressed by the magnitude of the fine that they were forced to pay under the terms of the peace of 241, and were determined to avenge their humiliating defeat. So they gave to Hamilcar Barca, who had been the defeated general in Sicily, the task of preparing for a new war. But because Sicily and the sea route to Italy were in Roman hands, he was compelled to make plans for an invasion of Italy from Spain, where he established colonies, raised an army from among the Spanish tribes and founded the town of New Carthage (Cartagena) as a naval base. Everything that Hamilcar did was driven by his resentment of all things Roman, and he even made his young son Hannibal swear a formal oath that he would hate Rome for ever. The Romans in their turn were suspicious of all this activity, but the Carthaginians argued that they were merely raising taxes from the Spanish towns to pay off their war debt. Another treaty was signed in 226: the Carthaginians agreed to expand no further north than the Ebro river, and the Romans agreed to make no moves south of it.

Five years later, at the age of twenty-six, Hannibal became the Carthaginian commander-in-chief. Remembering the oath he had sworn to his father, he immediately precipitated a crisis by laying siege to Saguntum, a town in Spain that lay about a hundred miles south of the Ebro, well within Carthage's sphere of influence, but also by chance an ally of Rome.

Did Saguntum become allied with the Romans before or after the signing of the treaty of 226? If before, had it been specifically excluded from the treaty's terms? If after, had the treaty been broken by the Romans? The facts have never been clear, but it is hard not to believe that Hannibal deliberately attacked the town in order to provoke war. As might have been expected, the citizens of Saguntum appealed to Rome for help. For a while the Romans did nothing, being preoccupied with their campaign against the Illyrian pirates; but when Saguntum fell to Hannibal in the spring of 218, they declared war on Carthage.

Hannibal's Invasion of Italy

Hannibal at once set in motion his invasion of Italy from the north. He had an immediate advantage because he had all his best troops with him already in Spain, and the Romans were not yet ready to face him. For the longer term, however, the Romans would theoretically have the advantage, because they had command of the sea and greater depths of reserves at home. Nevertheless, Hannibal hoped that, once he could make his way into Roman territory, his smaller numbers would be offset if he could persuade Rome's Italian allies to revolt and to join him.

Almost unopposed, he first crossed the Pyrenees, which separated Spain from Gaul; and then the river Rhone, where he had some difficulty ferrying over his elephants, which he used to carry the heaviest loads. He constructed a huge raft, covered it with turf to make it look like an extension of the bank, and tempted the bull-elephants onto it by the lure of a cow-elephant in heat; then he towed the highly unstable load across the river. It was worth the trouble because, when the local Gauls resisted him, the elephants were useful in scaring off any tribesmen who had planned ambushes and guerrilla attacks.

Still ahead were the Alps, by reputation daunting and in reality terrifying. The high Alpine passes were treacherous even in early summer. There were precipices and landslides, and the snow melted unevenly, so that the Carthaginians would fall through an apparently solid surface into freezing slush below. At the summit, Hannibal encouraged his exhausted troops in a famous speech: by getting this far, he said, they had in effect climbed over not just the Alps, but the very walls of Rome. Victory now lay in the hollow of their hands.

But the descent was even more difficult and dangerous than

the ascent, because it was so much steeper. At one point the path was completely blocked by a landslide, and the soldiers had to soak the rocks with a makeshift acid—their wine rations allowed to go sour—and then light bonfires to heat the rocks until they could be split with pickaxes. Losses of men (perhaps a third of the total), horses, mules and elephants were extremely heavy, and the army had to be given four days' rest in the sunny north Italian plain to regain its strength and its morale. The crossing of the Alps had occupied two weeks out of a total of nearly five months occupied by the advance from New Carthage.

The survivors recovered quickly and completely. Within a few more days the Carthaginians had marched south, engaged the Romans, and defeated them, mainly because of Hannibal's superior deployment of cavalry. Many of the Roman legionaries escaped, however, and a second and much more serious battle was fought in the following spring (217) on the shore of Lake Trasimene, about a hundred miles north of Rome in the Apennine mountains. Hannibal took up his position north of the lake on level ground, and waited there for the Roman consul Flaminius, who arrived from the south late in the evening but in time to catch sight of Hannibal's army across the water. Arrogant by nature, and goaded by his junior officers, who thought he was too cautious, Flaminius determined to attack Hannibal at dawn.

Even before it was fully light, Flaminius moved through the thick mist arising from the lake, marching his troops in a long column along the path between the lake and the mountains. When he had advanced too far along the path to turn back, the Carthaginian light infantry and cavalry, who had moved into new positions in the mountains overnight, attacked his flank, charging down the slope and taking him completely by surprise. For three hours the Romans, trapped between the mountains and the water, tried to fight their way out, so desperately and so savagely that they did not even notice an earthquake that rattled the ground on which they stood; but they were unable to regroup effectively because they could not hear their officers' orders nor see what they were doing in the mist. Fifteen thousand Romans were killed or, weighed down by their armor, drowned in the shallows, and Flaminius was murdered by his own disgruntled men. The rest straggled back to the city with the news of their terrible defeat.

The Senate did not panic. As they had before in moments of great crisis, they appointed a dictator, Quintus Fabius Maximus, who, after making dutiful sacrifices to appease what looked like the anger of the gods, developed an entirely new strategy. The Romans must not allow themselves to be tempted into any more pitched battles, because they could not afford any more casualties. Instead they would keep in constant contact with Hannibal, retreating before him but avoiding an actual clash, while they destroyed any food or equipment that might fall into Hannibal's hands. To the Romans this strategy was unpopular—it seemed pointless and cowardly—and indeed it was some time before it showed any success. But Fabius patiently kept on the move, often shifting his camp at night, always just out of the Carthaginians' reach but always within their view. That summer there were no more defeats, and as the Romans withdrew to the south, so Hannibal followed them, finding it harder to supply his troops as his lines of communication back to Spain became ever longer. His men began to grumble, even to whisper of mutiny.

During the winter, Fabius' term of office as dictator expired. The consuls began to get tired of delay, and looked for another opportunity to meet Hannibal in battle. They chose their spot on the plain at Cannae—low on the calf of the Italian boot—pinning their hopes on their infantry, which still outnumbered Hannibal's, and discounting their weakness in cavalry.

The Romans' initial charge broke through the Carthaginian center, but Hannibal's cavalry was biding its time along each wing and attacked them on both flanks and in the rear, using the same "double encirclement" maneuver that the Athenians had used at Marathon. The legions were surrounded and cut to pieces: fifty thousand Romans and allies were killed, including one of the consuls; five thousand were taken prisoner; and the rest scattered and fled into the surrounding countryside.

The next day at dawn, the Carthaginians came to collect the

spoils and look at the slaughter. Even they were appalled at what they had done. Thousands of Roman soldiers were dead; infantry and cavalry lay together where the chances of battle had brought them, or where they had tried to find a way to escape.

> *In some places the Carthaginians found wounded men still alive, covered in blood and trying to struggle to their feet after they had been brought back to consciousness by the morning chill. Some they finished off at once; others, with their legs nearly severed, had to beg to be put out of their misery, and stretched out their necks so that their throats could be cut. Some had suffocated themselves by lying face downward in holes that they had dug in the mud. One soldier from Africa was found still alive, but most of his face was missing; he lay under the body of a Roman who had died in the act of tearing at his enemy with his teeth.*

(Livy: *History*, xxii. 51)

At this crucial moment, Hannibal hesitated. Though urgently advised by his officers to mount an immediate attack on Rome itself, he decided to spend more time on sporadic raids in the south, evidently waiting for some of the allied towns to come over to his side. However, only Capua defected, and Hannibal set up a permanent base there. His second-in-command reproached him: "Hannibal, you know how to win a victory, but not how to use one."

Hannibal's indecision may have been caused by the Romans' own unbending attitude. The Senate and people did not despair after the battle of Cannae, while the Roman allies in Latium remained loyal and blocked Hannibal's way to the city. Their defeat had shown them, moreover, that Fabius' delaying tactics were, at least for the moment, the only successful method of keeping Hannibal in check. Though the two sides might be roughly equal in infantry, the Romans would not be able to defeat the Carthaginians until they had learned to overcome Hannibal's superiority in cavalry and could cut him off from his home base and from reinforcements.

Campaigns Abroad

The Carthaginian government, aware that Hannibal's chances of capturing Rome were poor as long as the Italian allies stood firm, now hoped to encourage hostility from outside Italy, so that the Romans would find themselves encircled by foreign enemies. But Carthage would not or could not give its own allies much effective support, and in this next stage of the war the Romans, operating abroad, did better then they had at home.

First, Roman forces made successful raids by land and sea on the Carthaginians still quartered in Spain, and many of the Spanish tribes came over to the Roman side. Though fighting continued for several years, the Roman grasp on Spain eventually tightened so much that Hannibal could no longer count on the overland route for supplies and reinforcements.

King Philip V of Macedonia, who was hostile to Rome because of its occupation of Illyria, had made an alliance with Carthage in 216. However, in subsequent skirmishes with Roman troops in northern Greece, Philip received no assistance from Carthage, and in the end was compelled to make a treaty with Rome.

Throughout the war, the towns of Sicily remained generally loyal, a mark of the efficiency with which Rome was governing its new province. But in 214 the city of Syracuse revolted after several months of internal dissension. The Romans sent a fleet and two legions (including some of the survivors of Cannae, who were given this opportunity to redeem themselves) to blockade Syracuse. Syracuse, although receiving very little Carthaginian help, held out for two years, thanks largely to the catapults and other gadgets designed by Archimedes, that famous philosopher from Alexandria who had claimed that if you gave him a lever he could move the earth, and who had run naked through the streets shouting "*Eureka*" (Greek for "I've got it") after he had discovered in his bath-tub the principle of displacement. In 212, Syracuse fell; and Archimedes, absorbed in a problem of geometry and thinking nothing of any danger, was surprised and killed by a Roman soldier. The southern route to Carthage was now more than ever securely in Roman hands.

The End of Hannibal's Campaign in Italy

Fabius was now consul; his delaying strategy had turned out now to be the right one, and the cognomen Cunctator (Delayer), which had at first been given him as an insult, now became a title of honor. As he kept Hannibal's army penned up in the south, Fabius was said to have saved the state. But Hannibal, on the other hand, became more and more depressed: for the Romans, despite their enormous losses at Trasimene and Cannae, seemed to have inexhaustible reserves. They had been successful in Spain and Sicily, and now, at the same time as they were blockading Syracuse, they laid siege to his base at Capua. Hannibal tried to draw off the besieging force by marching on Rome, but outside the city he learned that the Romans had raised yet another army to oppose him. And he caught wind of a rumor that had been leaked by the Senate in a masterly stroke of disinformation, that the land on which he was encamped had just been put up for auction, and that bidding was going through the roof.

In the face of such a display of Roman confidence, and doubtless remembering how he had passed up an earlier chance of capturing Rome after the battle of Cannae, Hannibal turned away. He seemed to have lost his nerve, and he did not even return to Capua, which fell to the Romans in the following year (213). It was, if not the beginning of the end, at least the end of the beginning.

Rome on the Offensive

Hannibal wandered about listlessly in Italy four more years, but had no more luck in winning over the Italian allies. In 207, his brother Hasdrubal broke out of Spain and made his way across the Alps with an army consisting mainly of Gallic mercenaries. But before he could join forces with Hannibal, Hasdrubal was caught between two Roman armies on the bank of the Metaurus river. He was comprehensively defeated, and his ambitious attempt to bring Hannibal reinforcements collapsed. It was the first time that the Romans had beaten a Carthaginian army in a major battle, and by their triumph, they not only effectively ended Hannibal's Italian campaign, but also turned the war in their favor.

The result of the battle of the Metaurus river was made doubly satisfactory by more news from Spain, where a brilliant young Roman general, Publius Cornelius Scipio, had wiped out the last pockets of Carthaginian resistance and captured New Carthage. He had learned the lesson of Cannae: the Roman legions must learn to maneuver more flexibly, and must coordinate their operations with the cavalry. By 206, Scipio was in complete control of Spain, which now became the third Roman province—later to be divided into Nearer and Further Spain.

At this point, Scipio wanted to take the war into Africa. Rome was now, he argued in the Senate, at the head of an impressive empire, but to retain its hold on it, Carthage must be defeated decisively on its own ground. However, he was opposed by Quintus Fabius Maximus, whose hesitation with victory on the horizon was not as farsighted as his caution on the brink of defeat. Hannibal, he warned, was still in Italy, and no one could anticipate the dangers of a campaign in Africa or anticipate the ferocity of the Carthaginian resistance. The job of Roman consuls and Roman armies was to defend Rome, not to go off adventuring in foreign lands.

In the end the Senate gave its approval to Scipio, who crossed over into Africa *via* Sicily, and set up a ring of bases around Carthage. The Carthaginians now regarded Scipio with the same apprehension that the Romans had regarded Hannibal a few years earlier; and they recalled Hannibal from Italy to organize the defense of Carthage.

In the summer of 202, the two armies lined up opposite each

other outside the village of Zama, near Carthage. However, Hannibal first requested a conference to explore the possibility of an armistice. He and Scipio, two of the most distinguished generals in history, faced each other in mutual admiration. Hannibal, without denying that he had been the original aggressor, and without expecting any favorable terms, asked simply for an end of the killing. But Scipio was determined that Hannibal must be punished, not forgiven, and the conference came to nothing. So Scipio became the first Roman general to face Hannibal in a formal battle since Cannae fourteen years before, and the only one ever to defeat him. Just as, in the first Punic war, the Romans had won by modifying Carthage's most effective weapon, the warship, so now Scipio (afterwards nicknamed Africanus) won the battle of Zama by adapting and improving upon Hannibal's own cavalry tactics.

Hannibal escaped unhurt from the battlefield, and persuaded the Carthaginian forces to surrender on the reasonable—and not retaliatory—terms that Scipio offered. The terms of the peace treaty required the Carthaginians to give up their ships and elephants, and to pay a fine that severely weakened their economy; in return the Romans agreed to withdraw from Africa. Carthage was to become a dependent ally of Rome and agreed to undertake no aggressive action against another state without the permission of the Senate.

The Victory of the Roman Republic

The war was over, and the Romans could sit back and congratulate themselves on a remarkable achievement. The steadiness and self-sacrifice of the members of their Confederacy had enabled them to wear down Hannibal's energy and will, while neither they nor their allies had ever seemed to doubt their eventual ability to withstand whatever the enemy might bring against them. Good roads and the excellent fortifications of the Italian towns had allowed the Roman armies to move quickly and rest safely even while Hannibal apparently had the upper hand. And they had found exactly the generals they needed in the two very different phases of the war: Quintus Fabius Maximus, whose patient defensive tactics had rescued them after the battle of Lake Trasimene; and Publius Cornelius Scipio, who had shown himself in Spain and Africa to be an aggressive commander as brilliant and ingenious as Hannibal at his best.

But most of all the war was a magnificent, grim demonstration of the Roman character. Neither the Senate nor the people, the crucial elements of the constitution, had been deterred by disaster nor distracted by triumph. During month after month of inactivity and the slow, dogged maneuvering that led at last to the final victorious push into Africa, they had never lost their poise or their belief in a common cause. The republic had enjoyed its finest hour.

6. The Challenges of Power

Foreign Policy 201 – 146 BC

At the end of the second Punic war Rome was the strongest state in the Mediterranean region, and during the next fifty years would not hesitate to flaunt its power in its relations with its neighbors, the so-called Hellenistic kingdoms. These were the remaining segments of Alexander the Great's empire, that were now ruled by the descendants of his generals: they included the confederacies and independent city-states of Greece, the Greek cities of Asia Minor, and in particular Macedonia, Syria and Egypt.

The Romans had already became embroiled in the complicated world of Macedonian and Greek politics, as a result of their earlier campaigns against the Illyrian pirates and against Hannibal's ally, Philip V of Macedonia. Now they went to war again against a still aggressive Philip, defeated him, and annexed Macedonia as a Roman province. But the Greek cities continued, as they had done throughout their history, to quarrel among themselves; and at last the entire area became so unstable that the Romans lost patience with all of them. As a warning to the rest, they sacked Corinth in 146, and the Greeks were lumped together as a Roman protectorate, which would eventually become the province of Achaia.

Meanwhile King Antiochus of Syria was interfering with the Greek cities in Asia Minor, which Rome had promised to defend. Despite the advice of Hannibal, who had fled to his court after the battle of Zama, Antiochus was defeated in 168, and the Romans were now recognized as a political and military force to be reckoned with. When one of Antiochus' successors made plans to invade Egypt (with whom Rome had a treaty), they were able to stop him cold by sending an envoy who simply drew a line in the desert sand and warned the Syrian king not to step across it.

The Romans now established Egypt, Syria and several of the

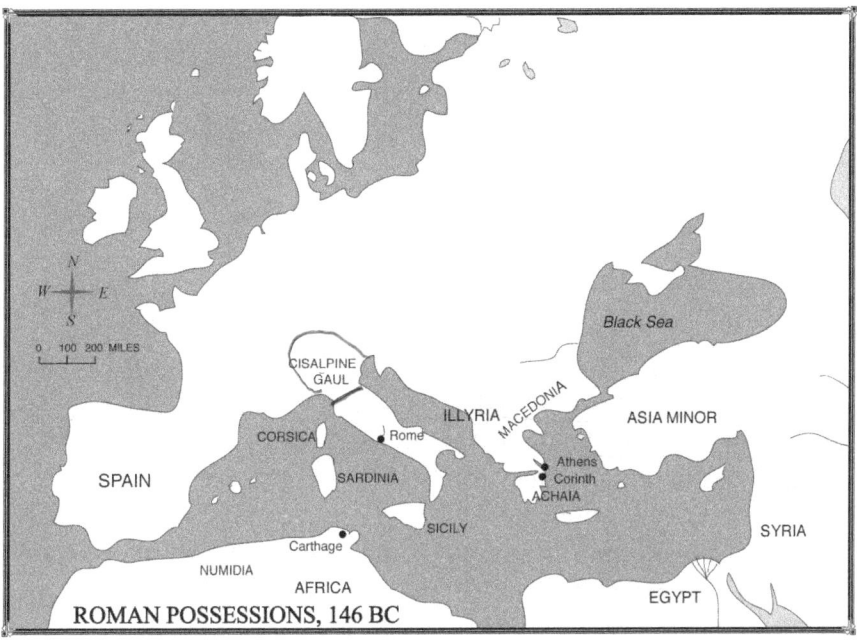

ROMAN POSSESSIONS, 146 BC

TERRITORY CONTROLLED BY THE ROMAN REPUBLIC, 146 B.C.

Provinces
Sicily
Sardinia and Corsica
Nearer and Further Spain (Hispania)
Macedonia
Africa

Protectorates (later provinces)
Illyria
Cisalpine Gaul
Greece (Achaia)

Client Kingdoms
Syria
Greek kingdoms in Asia Minor
Egypt
Numidia

states of Asia Minor as "client kingdoms"—independent allies of Rome who promised to defend Roman interests in the east in return for Roman support, and who could often function as a buffer zone between the barbarians and the provinces.

The Administration of the Provinces

The system that the Romans developed for governing their new provinces stemmed directly from the arrangements that already existed for Rome itself. At the end of their term of office in Rome, consuls and praetors would have their normal one-year *imperium* extended, by decree of the Senate, for an extra three years, during which time they would become the governor of a province. They would be known as proconsuls or propraetors, because in their provinces they would be officially acting *pro consule* or *pro praetore* (in the place of a consul or a praetor). Quaestors and other staff were added if they were required.

Foreign wars were from now on normally fought with armies led from the nearest province; therefore the most important and the most prestigious part of a governor's job was to command the military forces which were used to protect its borders. He was also the province's chief administrator, responsible for keeping the peace, for collecting taxes, and for constructing and maintaining public works such as temples, roads and bridges. But because he was not under the direct control of the Senate, nor subject to the veto of a tribune, as he would have been in Rome, a governor could behave in his province in ways that he might never do at home; he acted, in fact, almost like a king.

As Roman magistrates they still remained unpaid, and the temptation to plunder, extort or embezzle must have been very strong. To many Romans the governorship of a province became a highly desirable opportunity, not simply to satisfy their political ambition but to secure their financial future; and in fact they frequently ran for a consulship in Rome with the specific objective of being appointed afterwards to a province.

By the middle of the second century BC, rumors of financial

misbehavior were rife, and as a result the Senate in 149 set up a special court (the *quaestio de rebus repetundis*) to prosecute governors who were accused of corruption. However, since senators sitting on this court would be judging a member of their own class, and since they themselves might have in the past committed a similar offense or might do so in the future, the possibility of bias was clear. A cynical joke went into circulation: a governor could make enough in his first year in office to pay off the bribes that had got him the job, in the second year enough to pay off the bribes to ensure his acquittal by the court that would try him, and in the third year enough to live in comfort for the rest of his life. Nevertheless, the evidence of court records does not support the joke, and trials were rare enough to show that the Roman sense of honesty and honor remained strong, and that the system must on the whole have worked well. If nothing else, the establishment of Roman provinces and alliances brought comparative peace to the whole Mediterranean and Middle Eastern region for nearly five hundred years.

The Third Punic War: 149 – 146 BC

During the wars in the east, the Carthaginians had faithfully fulfilled their new obligations as Roman allies, including the provision of troops for Roman armies. But when they unilaterally declared war on the neighboring kingdom of Numidia, which had for a long time been harassing Carthage by raiding its territory, they also broke their obligation not to act as the aggressor against another state. Because Carthage had clearly been provoked, the matter might easily have been settled by negotiation, but for the faction in the Senate which still feared and hated Carthage. The faction was led by Marcus Cato, a conservative who as a matter of routine would loudly denounce all foreign powers as potential enemies, and had been for some time in the habit of ending any speech on any topic with the formula *"Carthago est delenda"* (Carthage must be destroyed).

Now Cato had found his rationale for another Punic war. The

Senate, with some reluctance, agreed to send an army to besiege Carthage, under the command of Scipio the grandson of Scipio Africanus, who is said to have wept when he saw the magnificence of the city he had been sent to conquer. When Carthage fell in 146—the same year as the sack of Corinth—its territory became the province of Africa, and Numidia a client kingdom.

Carthage itself was completely destroyed. The ground on which it stood was ploughed over, salt was sowed in its furrows and an eternal curse was laid upon it—a harsh punishment which can have satisfied few consciences except Cato's. Though the Carthaginians had technically broken the treaty, there was no reason to go to war with them again, and certainly none to wipe out their city. The incident did no credit to the Romans or to the spirit with which they had finished the second Punic war, for up to this point in their history the Romans had had no deliberately aggressive or imperialist policy. They had fought their wars essentially to consolidate what they already had, or to protect what had fallen almost accidentally under their control.

7. The Political and Social Results of the Punic Wars

Government

Cato perhaps had been wrong to instigate the destruction of Carthage, but he was not a fool. He and his more conservative colleagues were worried—correctly—about the dangers of trying to manage an empire that now extended all round the Mediterranean, with the institutions and practices which had originally been developed for a small homogeneous city-state. The more provinces Rome had, they argued, the more magistrates it needed to govern them; and the more magistrates it had, the less exclusive the Senate would become, and its moral authority would be weakened as it tried to deal with the new influences that now came crowding into Roman life.

The increasing need to extend the *imperium* of magistrates, whether to govern provinces or to command armies on lengthy campaigns, had led the Senate to disregard an old law that had prevented any official from being re-elected until he had been out of office for ten years. During the second Punic War, for instance, Quintus Fabius Maximus had been elected consul three years in a row, and Scipio had been either consul or proconsul for ten successive years. Just after the Punic wars, the Senate had put into place a set of rules called the *cursus honorum*: magistrates had to work their way up a ladder of successive offices, from quaestor to consul, with a minimum age fixed for holding each office. The Senate reasoned that to give a magistrate too much power, or to give it to him too soon, would encourage personal ambition rather then loyalty to the interests of the state. Their intentions were good: but the Senate never succeeded in enforcing the rules of the *cursus honorum* or indeed any of the other checks on individuals' use of their *imperium*. And this was one of the failures that, within a little more than a hundred and fifty years from the triumphant end of the Punic wars, would lead to the disintegration of the republic.

Citizens

From 264 to 146, Roman armies had been in action more or less constantly, especially since Hannibal's invasion, and the need for new recruits (who were drafted for the duration of hostilities only) had been steadily increasing. The new importance of the cavalry, whose members had to be rich enough to provide and care for their own horses, had led to greater political influence for a class of prosperous men (called the *equites*, the Latin word for horsemen), who were not in the Senate, and who had made their money in business rather than from land. The infantry, on the other hand, were drawn from farms and workshops, from all but the very poorest citizens. Some had been conscripted at the time in their lives when they would normally have been thinking of marrying and setting up their own households; others had just started families, which had then been forced to carry on without them. During and after the wars, there was a steep increase in celibacy and divorce: many young men became used to unmarried life and did not particularly want to change their status, and many older men found that their wives had grown away from them and their children did not know them.

And of course many thousands of Romans had been killed in action—more than sixty thousand at Lake Trasimene and Cannae alone—or had died abroad. Often a family's entire male line had been wiped out. Many women (allowed to possess property according to the laws of the Twelve Tables) had inherited land or money and were not only enjoying a comfortable life of independence, but were making important financial decisions and managing large estates. They then began to appear more frequently in public, at religious ceremonies or at the games, while the daughters of noble families were often given the same education as the sons: in Rome groups of women routinely gathered for intellectual and political discussion. But even this new freedom for women did not afford them a new political role, except as movers and shakers behind the scenes.

At the other end of the social scale, however, there was eco-

Country life: a farmer hands over a bull and a ram for sacrifice to one of the country gods. (Art Resource)

nomic disruption. Demobilized soldiers, returning home, often found that their farms had failed through lack of proper attention, or that their land had been sold and absorbed into someone else's. Large estates (called *latifundia*) thus grew even larger at the expense of the traditional small farms. Since it was more economical to use slave labor, there were few jobs on the latifundia available for the poorer citizens, nor any land left for them to rent.

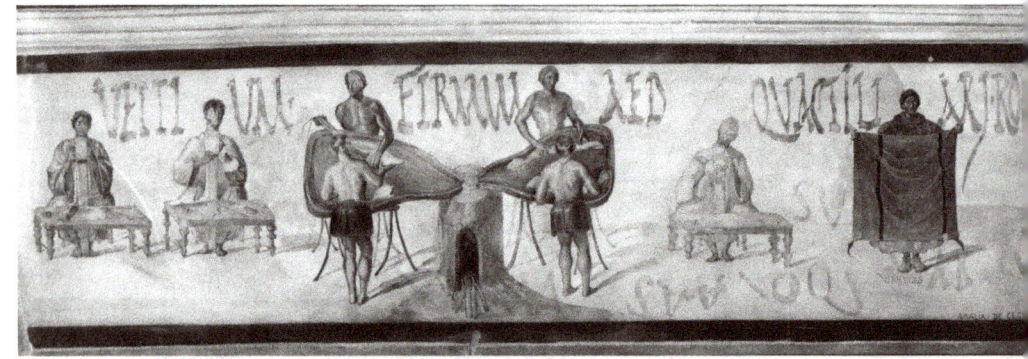

A workshop in the city: craftsmen preparing lengths of material to be made into clothing. (Art Resource)

Displaced and dispossessed farmers began to drift into the towns, and especially to Rome, where again they found a glut of cheap labor. Eventually the unemployed began to outnumber the craftsmen and shopkeepers who had originally made up the urban population, and formed a large, restless underclass, which the Senate tried to keep contented by the distribution of free or government-subsidized wheat—much of it imported from the new province of Africa—or distracted by lavish gladiatorial shows and chariot races.

Entertainment and subsidies were not available, however, to the Italian allies, who had supported the Romans so long, so faithfully and so well. They had won no profits from the war and no perks; they had no vote which they might have been able to use in a campaign to alleviate their plight. Quietly, and tactfully to begin with, they began to look for support for a change in their status, to press for full Roman citizenship.

Slaves

As was always to be expected in the ancient world, conquests and annexations led to prisoners of war, and prisoners were forced to become slaves. Though a body of law existed that was designed to look after the slaves' interests, the Romans did not question the institution of slavery itself. In Rome, as in any of the great civilizations of Europe, Africa or Asia, slavery was an accepted, natural part of life, which did not seriously attract the attention of moral philosophers or social reformers until the arrival of Christianity, some two hundred years in the future.

Roman slaves fell into two distinct categories: domestic slaves, and field slaves who worked on the farms, especially on the *latifundia*. The latter were badly treated by any standard, because they were expendable and their labor was cheap. They were usually kept in chains, were miserably housed and fed, and worked under the whip. By contrast, the slaves in private households were by law counted as members of the family, and came under the authority of the *paterfamilias* exactly like his children. Household slaves were paid a regular small wage for their services, and many of them invested this money until they could buy their freedom. Alternatively, some were freed by their masters as a reward for long years of faithful service. These *liberti* (freedmen) could not become citizens themselves, but their children automatically received full citizen rights, including the right to vote.

The most important result, however, of the influx of slaves who would give them easily available help in all their household chores, and often waited on them hand and foot, was that freeborn Romans lost one of their most revered ideals—self-sufficiency. The richer they were, the more slaves they could afford to keep and the greater risk they ran of becoming completely pampered and dependent.

Greeks

Rome's first contact with the Greeks had occurred when, as a result of the war with Pyrrhus of 280, it had absorbed the Greek colonies of southern Italy into the Roman federation. They had been exposed to further Greek influences during the campaigns in Sicily, Macedonia and Illyria during the Punic wars, and even more as Greece itself came under Roman protection after 146. Disseminated by an enthusiastic group of nobles led by the younger Scipio and known as the "Scipionic Circle", Greek ideas now spread inexorably into every corner of Roman life, sometimes resented or feared as a dilution of traditional Roman gravity and seriousness, sometimes welcomed as a softening, lightening influence. *Graecia capta ferum victorem cepit,* wrote the poet Horace: Once captured, Greece has taken its rough conqueror captive.

The Senate had traditionally been committed not only to maintaining its own oligarchic power, but also to guiding the entire citizen body towards what it saw as a common good: a necessary resistance to change at every level of the state, preserved officially and unofficially by the examples of the *mos maiorum*. But now from Greece came the same kind of liberal talk that had once shaped Athenian democracy: talk about the freedom of individual citizens, the right to debate and to question the *status quo*. At home the impregnable wall of the Senate, which had sheltered the Roman people through the most critical moments of its history, would begin to crumble before the exploratory chipping of both altruistic and ambitious individuals. And abroad, in the provinces of the empire, it now became possible to understand in practical terms Alexander the Great's vision of the world as a pattern of infinite variety within a unity built on shared political and social values.

A significant number of the new slaves were Greeks or Macedonians, who brought Greek morals and manners directly into Roman households. Under their instruction, more luxurious habits of diet and daily living began to take hold in Roman houses—and this further encouraged Roman self-indulgence. The Senate reacted by proposing new laws which limited expense on clothes, jewelry, carriages—even on slaves themselves—but of course the measures had absolutely no effect.

Greek slaves who were sophisticated and well-read (more literate perhaps than their masters) often went beyond domestic service and were set to tutor the children of the house; later, schools on the Greek model came into fashion among rich families. So the *paterfamilias* was gradually distanced from the education of his children, and his children from the pressures of the old-fashioned conservatism: their Latin became sprinkled with Greek words, and then they began to learn the Greek language, until fluency in Greek became not only the mark of a good education, but also an essential tool for diplomacy and trade.

With the Greek language came increasing familiarity with Greek art and literature. As they had always been in Athens, the poems of Homer became the core of the curriculum, along with Greek drama, history and philosophy. The study of Greek oratory by Roman lawyers and politicians greatly influenced their style of public speaking and forensic argument, and Greek literature served as models for a new generation of Roman authors. The earliest extant examples of Latin literature consist of little more than fragments of songs, official inscriptions, long instructional treatises (Cato wrote one on agriculture) and clumsy burlesques. Now, under Greek influence, Plautus and Terence wrote plays in imitation of the "new comedy" of Menander—tales of ingenious slaves who lead their masters through a trial of mistaken identities, new-found loves and long-lost relations—on which in turn have been based Shakespearean comedies, Broadway musicals such as *A Funny Thing Happened on the Way to the Forum* and the Jeeves stories of P.G. Wodehouse. Latin versions (now lost) of Greek epics began to appear, and, later, Lucretius wrote a long poem in the epic meter called *De Rerum Natura* (The Nature of the Universe). Following the Athenian philosopher Epicurus, Lucretius rejected conventional religion and proposed a mechanical arrangement of atoms as an explanation of the workings of the cosmos. Although he was not in fact a convinced atheist, his apparent undermining of Roman reverence for the gods was another blow to the ascendancy of the *mos maiorum*.

PART II
THE END OF THE REPUBLIC

8. The Gracchi

Tiberius Gracchus: Tribune 133 BC

The daughter of Scipio Africanus was one of those who had her children brought up by Greek tutors in the fifty years following the Punic wars. The elder of her two sons, Tiberius Sempronius Gracchus, was early exposed to the Greek idea that it was the duty of a citizen to question the political *status quo*; and despite—or perhaps because of—his aristocratic background, his sympathies lay with the underprivileged. He was particularly aware of the misery of the dispossessed farmers; and he once remarked that Roman soldiers, after being exhorted for so long by the Senate to fight for the glories and traditions of their city, had in the end discovered that they had merely been defending the incomes of the rich. The conquerors of the world, he said, had no place to call their own.

In 133 Tiberius Gracchus was elected tribune of the plebs. Hoping to make more land available to veterans and other homeless citizens, he proposed legislation to limit the size of the largest estates and distribute the surplus in allotments to the poor. The senators, whose holdings would of course have been directly affected if this radical proposal were to become law, might still have accepted the measure as a personal sacrifice for the general good. But Tiberius assumed that they would be universally opposed to it, and therefore took his bill directly to the assembly of the people without consulting them.

His move was not strictly illegal, but it ran contrary to the long tradition that legislation debated in the assemblies should receive the Senate's prior approval. The Senate, therefore, anxious about its ancient prerogatives, persuaded another tribune to veto the bill. To do this was entirely within his constitutional rights, but Tiberius immediately persuaded the people to vote to depose him.

> *"A tribune of the people is sacrosanct,"* he argued, *"and his person is inviolable, because the tribune's sacred duty is to guard and protect the people. But if he departs from this duty, if he oppresses the people or tries to tell them what to do, or prevents them from exercising their right to vote—then he should not expect to receive any honors or privileges, because he has not performed the duties in exchange for which the honors and privileges were granted to him in the first place... A tribune who did such things would be a bad tribune; a tribune who fails to support the people is not a tribune at all"...*
>
> *"A king—who holds complete power in his own person—holds a sacred office and is under the protection of the gods. But this did not prevent the citizens of Rome from deposing Tarquinius Superbus when he did wrong. As a result of the crimes of that one man, the ancient monarchy of Rome was abolished... A tribune cannot remain inviolate when he offends the people who gave him his inviolability; the people made him, and the people can undo him."*
>
> (Plutarch: *Life of Tiberius Gracchus* 15)

To override his colleague's veto was clearly wrong, but because of it Tiberius' bill was passed, and the land was redistributed: but Tiberius, with further reforms in mind, again challenged tradition and the Senate by standing for election to a second successive tribunate. The move was not against the law (the tribunes were not subject to the rules of the *cursus honorum*) but again it was unprecedented, and again the senators were upset. But the final straw came when the client-king of Pergamum in Asia Minor died and in his will bequeathed his kingdom to Rome. Pergamum became the province of Asia, and Tiberius put to the people a proposal that some of its enormous wealth should be used to cover the start-up costs of the newly settled farmers. But this was none of the people's business: the Senate's responsibility for foreign and financial affairs was indisputable.

Senators now saw Tiberius' interference as intolerable, and they could no longer contain their anger at his affronts. A group of them, armed with clubs, made their way into the assembly. Both sides lost their tempers; fighting broke out and in an appalling scene, such as had not happened since the expulsion of the kings, Tiberius and hundreds of his supporters were beaten to death and their bodies tossed into the river.

Events of Roman Revolution
133 BC – 31 BC

Gaius Gracchus: Tribune 123 BC

Exactly ten years later, Tiberius' younger brother Gaius became tribune, and he continued his brother's campaign to redistribute land to the poor. He also set out to give political power to the middle class, the equites, who had become very influential because of their wealth. He proposed to enroll three hundred of them in the Senate; but when this came to nothing, he had the people pass a law that allowed the *equites* to take over from the Senate the control of the jury-courts, particularly the court which dealt with the cases of provincial governors charged with extortion. This was a poor idea in the first place—it merely led to charges of bias in one direction being switched to charges of bias in the other, and did no more than set the Senate and the equites against each other.

But once more the senators were offended, and they determined to get rid of Gaius before he could threaten their prerogatives further. They wrecked his future political career by spreading discreditable rumors about him, and then, in a street scuffle, one of Gaius' supporters killed a slave belonging to one of the consuls. At this, the senators became irrationally alarmed, and they passed a measure called *senatus consultum ultimum ut consules viderent ne res publica detrimentum caperet* (an emergency decree of the senate, instructing the consuls to see to it that the state come to no harm). The decree gave the Senate's moral support to whatever steps the consuls might find necessary to keep the peace—and those steps, it was implied, included the use of force. In protest against the extraordinary powers apparently given to the consuls, the plebeians rioted. Three thousand of Gaius' supporters were arrested and executed, while Gaius himself, despairing that the situation had slipped entirely out of his control, committed suicide.

The Legacy of the Gracchi

The calm of the streets of Rome had been disastrously shattered, and the Gracchi, not surprisingly perhaps, became martyrs.

The Roman people... commissioned statues of the brothers and had them openly displayed, and the places where they had lost their lives were consecrated. The people would sacrifice there the first fruits of every season's harvest...

Their mother Cornelia is said to have borne her loss with calm nobility. She remarked that it was entirely apt that shrines should be set up where her sons had died... It was wonderful to hear her, later, talk about them without any tears or show of mourning. Rather she would discuss their successes and their failures as if she were telling stories about the dead heroes of legend. Some people thought that old age or great grief had muddled her mind or hardened her heart, but they themselves were the ones devoid of feeling; they could not understand that a stern character and a strict upbringing will provide sufficient strength for anyone to overcome any sorrow.

(Plutarch: *Life of Gaius Gracchus* 18)

The Gracchi had proposed effective or at least well-intended reforms. So what had gone wrong? Their primary motive, perhaps, was to show that the will of the people ought not be dependent on the approval of a senatorial oligarchy—that the Roman constitution should be democratic in fact and not just in theory. But if their education had made them think wistfully of the thorough-going democracy of Periclean Athens, they should also have been aware of Plato's condemnation of that democracy, and his conviction that ordinary citizens were not wise enough to make correct decisions. Certainly the Roman assemblies of the second century BC were not as responsible as they had been in the great days of the Punic wars: the more the city became swamped with unemployed veterans without political experience, the less the likelihood of sound judgment in matters requiring compromise or patience. But the Gracchi had hardly acted responsibly themselves: Tiberius had failed to consult the Senate according to the *mos maiorum,* and had overridden the veto of a tribune; and both of them had tried to undermine the Senate's constitutional role.

The Senate, then, had been provoked, perhaps deliberately; but even so, the Senate's reaction to their provocation was certainly not an example of the restraint and good sense that they had demonstrated in the past. When it had most needed to be cool and imaginative, it had descended to the level of the most unruly members of the city mob. It had allowed itself to be unnerved by popular agitation, and the people had sensed its weakness. The effectiveness of violence rather than due legal process had become clear to both sides.

9. Marius and Sulla

Marius' Campaigns in Africa and Gaul

The irregular careers of Tiberius and Gaius Gracchus, and the agitation in the streets of Rome, had at least only affected domestic politics. But during the next generation the illegal machinations of generals and provincial governors, supported by the people acting against rather than with the Senate, ceased to be merely a matter of concern and instead began to pose a real threat to the stability of the state.

The first crisis was precipitated by a member of the *equites*, Gaius Marius. As a young man he had attracted some attention while serving in the army of Scipio, the grandson of the general who had defeated Hannibal in 202:

> *His general noticed him because of his courage, and because he had not complained when discipline was tightened up in reaction to the self-indulgent habits that the soldiers had adopted. There is a story too that he had beaten an enemy in single combat while his general was watching. He was well rewarded for his feat; and later, at a dinner party, when the conversation turned to the topic of leadership... somebody asked Scipio where the Romans would find another general such as himself. And Scipio put his arm around Marius, who was sitting next to him, and said, "Perhaps this is your man."*

(Plutarch: *Life of Marius* 3)

Subsequently he had been elected praetor and had then been sent to Spain as its governor, where again he did very well. In 107, although he was a *novus homo*, he was elected consul—but after his election the people ignored the Senate's prerogative of appointing provincial governors and added a special condition insisting that Marius, after his term of office, should be sent to the province of Africa as its proconsul.

The need for a competent commander in Africa had arisen because of a quarrel over the succession to the throne of the client kingdom of Numidia. In the fighting some Roman merchants had been killed and the Romans demanded a retaliatory attack. With some difficulty the pretender, Jugurtha, was captured and brought to trial in Rome on the charge that he had bribed certain Roman officials; but he wriggled out of his embarrassment by more bribery and left Rome with the cynical remark: "As long as you can find a buyer, everything in Rome is for sale." As soon as he arrived back in Numidia, however, he began to cause more trouble, and the Romans, under pressure from the *equites* who wanted a free hand to continue their trading operations, determined to be rid of him. So Marius went to Africa and made short work of him—a trivial enough affair but for the dangerous precedent of the people's bypassing of the Senate's right to select the governors of provinces.

But in 104 the people did exactly the same thing again. Having elected Marius consul once more—illegally at that, because ten years had not passed since his previous consulship— they simultaneously awarded him, again without the consent of the Senate, the command in the province of Cisalpine Gaul, which had been invaded by migrating tribes from Germany who now threatened Italy itself. Desperate fighting continued for three years, and for three years in succession Marius was re-elected consul, while the Senate's protests were silenced by the threat of mob violence.

When Marius finally defeated the German tribes, the people believed that he had saved Rome as surely as Camillus had saved it from the Gauls nearly three hundred years before. Hugely popular, he returned to Rome and was rewarded with a triumph—the celebratory parade voted by the Senate on rare occasions for a general who had particularly distinguished himself. The victorious army would march through the streets of the city, with prisoners and plunder on display, trumpets and flutes playing and the general bringing up the rear in his chariot.

By 100, Rome seemed safe and Marius was elected consul

for the sixth time. Once more the mobs came out, to force the Senate to approve the foundation of colonies and grants of land for the veterans—and this time Marius' soldiers joined in. But the riots were embarrassing to Marius himself, who had no political ambitions and did not wish to be seen condoning the behavior of the mob now that he was no longer seeking a military command. Once calm was restored in the streets, he retired to his country house.

Fragment of a relief sculpture celebrating a triumph: head of a soldier. (Photograph © 2004 Museum of Fine Arts, Boston)

Marius' Army Reforms

Marius' victories had been won in part by his own leadership in battle, but mainly because of his radical re-organization of the Roman army. He had ended the old system of drafting soldiers only for the duration of hostilities, and formed a professional standing army which was open to everyone, including the poorest social class, the *proletarii*. For greater flexibility, the legion, consisting at full strength of 6,000 men, was subdivided into smaller units, of which the smallest was the century (100 men), commanded by an experienced, hardened centurion who had risen through the ranks.

The infantry were for the first time uniformly equipped and armed: the short jabbing sword remained unchanged, but the *pilum* (throwing spear), was modified by a point which broke off either inside a wound or on contact with the ground, so that it could not be thrown back. On the march the soldiers carried their own entrenching tools so that at night their camp could be protected with a rampart and a ditch. With their full kits on their backs, they were popularly known as "Marius' mules."

In addition, each legion was given its own *signum* (from which the English *ensign* is derived) or standard. A standard served the same function as regimental colors: it was a symbol of the legion's identity and morale, as well as a highly visible mark round which the troops could rally during battle. It was a long pole topped with various decorative attachments—including the number of the legion, the letters SPQR surrounded by a laurel wreath, and a bronze *aquila* (eagle). Standards were closely guarded, and if one was lost or captured, the legion and the general were considered to be disgraced as badly as if they had been captured themselves.

The reforms were extremely successful in improving military effectiveness, mobility and morale, but there were dangers hidden within them. The new professional soldiers, who came mainly from the most underprivileged and neglected levels of society, came to believe that they were fighting not so much for Rome as for their general. It was, after all, he who recruited them, he who paid them with cash bonuses and a share of the plunder from captured towns and defeated armies, and he who had to request a foot-dragging Senate to make the allotments of farmland which were the only pensions they received. The soldiers' loyalty could no longer be taken for granted, and once Marius had established the precedent of having the people rather than the Senate choose who should command the armies, many of their generals felt no particular commitment to the Senate.

The Italian (or Social) War: 90 BC

Since the end of the Punic wars, the question of citizenship for the Italian allies had barely been seriously considered, let alone answered—but it had not gone away. Neither the Senate nor the people were enthusiastic about extending the franchise. The Senate felt it would lose whatever control it still maintained over the deliberation of the assemblies, if the members of the assemblies came from ever more varied backgrounds and whose points of view and demands could be less easily anticipated or satisfied; the people, on the other hand, feared for their perquisites, such as free or subsidized grain, if they were to be distributed among a larger citizen body. Therefore such few proposals as there were to give the vote to the allies had routinely failed, even as the allies increasingly complained that they had to fight for Rome without Roman rights. At last, in 90, the Italians rose in open revolt.

The Italians were mostly experienced soldiers and their leaders had organized them well, so well that the Romans themselves only slowly gained the upper hand in the fighting. Only after considerable loss of life on both sides, however, did the Senate finally decide to recognize the justice of the Italians' cause, and advised the tribunes to propose laws that would grant full citizenship to all the Italians.

The people of Italy still lived in their own towns under their own local governments, but now they were also Romans, with the right to vote, to involve themselves in the decisions of the assembly, and to embrace all the privileges and opportunities that Rome offered to its citizens. In practice, of course, most Italians seldom found the time to travel to Rome to exercise their privileges, and it would be a long time before local polling stations were set up in the towns, or before Italians were elected to office or became members of the Senate. Nevertheless, from this moment, Rome was no longer a city, but a nation.

Marius *versus* Sulla

There had been few bright spots for the Roman army in the course of the Italian war, but one of them was the performance of an officer who had also served with distinction under Marius in Africa, Lucius Cornelius Sulla. He was of noble ancestry but had grown up poor, with a purple birthmark on his face that evidently made him look like "a mulberry sprinkled with cornmeal." Later he inherited a fortune from his father's mistress, a Greek prostitute, but he remained prickly and self-conscious, always looking for slights despite his growing military reputation.

He was elected praetor in 93 and consul in 88; and at the end of his term he was appointed governor of the province of Asia, in order to deal with the imperial ambitions of Mithridates, king of Pontus. Mithridates had without provocation invaded Asia and in a single night (subsequently known as the "Asiatic vespers") had massacred 80,000 of its Roman residents, mainly merchants and their families. Now he was threatening to push on into Greece, and Sulla's instructions from the Senate were to get rid of him.

But when Sulla arrived in Brundisium and was preparing to embark his army for the voyage across the Adriatic, a tribune, perhaps looking for the support of the new Italian citizens against the aristocratic Sulla, suddenly proposed that the command be given instead to Marius. It was an absurd suggestion at best. Marius was old: he had retired before the Italian war and had seen no action for more than ten years—and his appointment would in any case have been illegal. Sulla was outraged, and he had no difficulty in persuading his army to turn back and seize control of Rome—the first of a series of examples, foreshadowed by Marius' reforms, of armies acting on behalf of their generals rather than of the state. Marius fled, and Sulla set off once again to Greece.

But as soon as Sulla's back was turned, Marius, swayed by foolish friends and by a fortune-teller who had prophesied that he would be consul seven times, returned to Rome. Half-crazy with a ruthless and irrational desire for revenge, he had many of Sulla's supporters murdered, and got his seventh consulship; but he died a few days later.

Sulla as Dictator: 83 – 79 BC

After two quick victories, Sulla forced Mithridates to agree to withdraw from the territory that he had overrun. But he did not finally defeat him, because he was in a hurry to return to Rome, and instead of leaving his legions in his province, he brought them back into Italy with him. He captured Rome once more, after some bloody street-fighting; and the Senate, anxious to see an end of the confusion, appointed him dictator—but not a dictator of the traditional kind that had last been used in the war against Hannibal. Instead of having a six-month limit, Sulla's dictatorship was for an indefinite term, with a specific mandate to "restore the republic." At once he initiated a program of "proscriptions": lists of his political opponents were posted in the forum, and those who were proscribed were forced to leave the city or be murdered without reprisal. Their property was then confiscated, ostensibly for redistribution to Sulla's veterans.

> *Proscriptions took place not only in Rome, but also in the Italian countryside. Nowhere was there a safe haven—not in the sanctuary of a temple, or in a private house. Men were stabbed in their wives' arms, children in their mothers'. Some died because they were considered a danger to the state, others because they were personally disliked by the dictator—but the great majority met their ends simply because they were rich. Even those*

who actually did the killing began to say that it was really a man's house, or his gardens, or his private baths, that had done him in.

(Plutarch: *Life of Sulla* 31)

Sulla proceeded with a series of reforms, which were mainly intended to weaken the tribunes and strengthen the Senate. He increased the number of senators to six hundred, and included all ex-magistrates, so that the people could feel that they had a hand in determining the Senate's membership, and would thus be less likely to challenge its authority. He further reinstated the very rules that he and Marius had so often broken in order to attain their power: the ban on re-election to any office until ten years had elapsed, the regulations of the *cursus honorum*, the Senate's control over provincial appointments. And he forbade any governor to leave his province, or lead his army out of his province, without the permission of the Senate.

Sulla's dictatorship lasted little more than three years, and in 79 he resigned and went off to live on his estate. Like Solon, he may have decided that if his new constitution was sound, it should be able to survive without him; he may have feared assassination by enemies who suspected that he wanted to make himself a king; or he may simply have felt old and tired and sick. After a few months in the country, he died.

10. Crassus, Pompey and Cicero

Spartacus and the Slaves' Revolt: 72 BC

Slavery had by now become an entirely accepted part of Roman life, and since the Punic wars, the presence of slaves on the *latifundia* had caused as significant a change in society as had slaves in private houses. The large number of field slaves was one of the main reasons why the city came to be filled with unemployed farmers and farm laborers who could so easily be formed into a mob and manipulated for their own devices by unscrupulous politicians. But despite their importance to the agricultural economy, the slaves were usually badly, even inhumanely, treated; and in 72 they revolted. They were led by a gladiator called Spartacus, evidently an organizer of genius, who formed them into a disciplined army of seventy thousand, with a base on the slopes on Mount Vesuvius, about a hundred miles south of Rome.

Though Spartacus himself was a Greek, most of the rebels were from Gaul, and Spartacus' original plan was to lead them across the northern border so that they could all go home. The consuls attempted to cut off their march, but without success: the slaves were victorious in half-a-dozen battles. But in the end they were rounded up by Marcus Crassus, in civilian life a banker who had made himself enormously rich during Sulla's proscriptions. The revolt was not entirely without result: it led to a definite improvement in conditions on the *latifundia*, though the price was high. Spartacus was killed, and six thousand captured slaves were crucified along the length of the Appian Way as an example to the rest.

Crassus might have been the hero of the hour, but right at the end of the revolt the governor of Spain returned from his province to mop up the last of the fugitives. His name was Gnaeus Pompeius (usually anglicized as Pompey), who had at one time been a lieutenant of Sulla's. Since then he had ingratiated himself with the Senate, who had quite irregularly appointed him proconsul in Spain even though he had never held office of any kind—thus showing that they were not going to take any notice of the *cursus honorum* or any other of Sulla's reforms if it did not suit them. Pompey and Crassus quarreled bitterly over which of them should take the credit for the defeat of the slaves' revolt; but they buried their differences and stood together for the consulship of 70. Neither of them was technically eligible: Crassus was too young, and Pompey had still never been a magistrate in Rome. But the Senate was intimidated into allowing the election when they both refused to disband their armies.

Pompey in the East

After an uneventful year as consul, Pompey soon achieved extraordinary office again: in 67 he was given special *imperium* to deal with the Mediterranean pirates who were seriously damaging Roman trade. He was given no time limit, but he wiped them out in a spectacular naval campaign in a single summer. In the next year, 66, he was given similar powers against Mithridates, who, having recovered from his defeat by Sulla, was again threatening the eastern provinces. This time he was not so lucky: Pompey trapped him inside a fort and besieged him there until he committed suicide.

Pompey now took preventive measures so that nuisances like Mithridates could not give any further trouble in the east. He drafted treaties of friendship with the remaining Hellenistic monarchs so that a ring of client kingdoms would separate Roman possessions from the dangerous Parthian empire in Persia and Mesopotamia (modern Iran and Iraq); and he proposed the creation of two new provinces, whose taxes would produce as much income as all the other provinces combined, as well as providing pensions for Pompey's retired soldiers. By making these proposals (which were known as his "Eastern Settlement"), Pompey had shown himself a brilliant administrator as well as a great soldier; and, as he was supposed to do by law, he now returned to Rome in order to lay them before the Senate for their formal ratification.

Catiline's Conspiracy: 63 BC

Pompey's arrival was not quite as triumphant as he might have hoped. Crassus still resented his role in the slave revolt, and was now vaguely insinuating that Pompey, with his new power gone to his head, wanted to set himself up as a king. Further, he found his achievements ignored amidst the excitement arising from the recent consulship of Marcus Cicero, a *novus homo* who had earlier supported the establishment of his special commands against the pirates and Mithridates. As the consul for 63, Cicero had overthrown a conspiracy to take over the state by a group of disgruntled nobles led by Catiline, whom he had defeated in the election. He had learned the details of the plot from the mistress of one of the conspirators, and had been able to pounce at the crit-

Nineteenth century painting by Cesari Maccari: *"Cicero and Catiline in the Senate."* (Art Resource)

red white blue is in the sky summers in your hair baby heavens in your eyes im your national anthem

ical moment. Catiline fled from Rome and was killed, but not before the rest of the conspirators had been arrested and put to death. Cicero himself made the laconic announcement of their fate. "*Vixerunt!*" he said. "Their lives are finished."

The conspiracy had in fact been poorly planned and poorly executed; it is remembered only because of Cicero's famous and impassioned speeches against Catiline in the Senate. But Cicero was convinced that he had saved the state from populist anarchy, and he began an energetic campaign to persuade the conflicting interests in Roman politics to forget their differences and to restore the old republican ideal of cooperation between the Senate and the people. It was an unrealistic and romantic dream, because the Senate, having failed so often to keep its own rules, had lost much of its traditional respect, as well as its ability to stand up to popular agitation.

11. The First Triumvirate

The Formation of the Triumvirate: 59 BC

Cicero's appeals were one thing, but Crassus' hints about Pompey's desire to be king turned out to be a great deal more significant, because the Senate appeared to take them seriously and therefore decided not to ratify his Eastern Settlement. Pompey was furious, and began to cast about for anyone who might be willing to join forces with him in forcing the Senate's hand. He remembered a former admirer of his, Gaius Julius Caesar, a noble who was connected by marriage with Marius. He had already been praetor and was now governor of Spain; and he too was having difficulties with the Senate. He could not win from them permission to stand *in absentia* for the consulship of 59—as governor he was not allowed to leave his province without their approval—nor a promise of another provincial command afterwards.

Caesar was therefore entirely willing to ally himself with Pompey, and to seal the deal he arranged for Pompey to marry his daughter Julia. Along with Caesar came Crassus, who presumably had decided that it would be safer to be with Pompey than against him, and was interested in seeing what tax breaks could be engineered for his business friends in Asia. The three of them formed what would be known to historians as the First Triumvirate, though they themselves called it simply an *amicitia*—a friendship. It was an informal, quite unconstitutional pact, whose members threatened shamelessly to use force if the Senate did not give them what they wanted.

The Senate quickly caved in under pressure from the triumvirate: Caesar was allowed to run for consul in 59 and was duly elected. Then he ignored the protests of his fellow consul—cynics called his term "the consulship of Julius and Caesar"—and smartly put through measures which would give his friends what they were demanding: the ratification of Pompey's Eastern

Settlement, with grants of land for his veterans, and changes in the law to benefit Crassus' cronies. For himself, he extracted from the Senate the guarantee of a special five-year command in Cisalpine Gaul, where he had recognized an opportunity to fulfill an ambition which had been with him for some time:

> *It is said that one day, when Caesar was a very young man in Spain, he was spending a day off-duty in reading a biography of Alexander the Great. He looked up from his book and sat lost in thought; and then he started to sob. His friends asked him what the matter was. "It's enough to make anyone cry," he said. "Look at how many countries Alexander had already conquered when he was my age—but so far I have done nothing worthwhile at all."*
>
> (Plutarch: *Life of Julius Caesar* 11)

Caesar in Gaul

The Gauls who lived on the far side of the Alps (Transalpine Gaul) had recently requested assistance in settling a border dispute with a migrating tribe from Switzerland. It was important for the Romans to maintain control of this area, because the route between Italy and Spain passed through it. However, Caesar had no intention of returning to his province once he had dealt with the immediate problem: for he had conceived the first truly imperialist enterprise in Roman history—a grand plan to conquer the whole of Gaul.

The detailed story of Caesar's Gallic adventure is contained in his own account, *De Bello Gallico* (On the Gallic War). In this memoir he describes how he divided and conquered the country by swift forced marches across the countryside in all directions, and by dashing military victories. His campaigns are still remembered: on a plain in Brittany alignments of prehistoric monoliths are said by local residents to be one of Caesar's legions turned to stone. In 55, when the tribes in northern Gaul revolted and had to be reconquered, he decided to invade Britain, because the rebels had a base there for training their forces. But he was beaten back by the courage of the blue-painted natives, the British weather and his own ignorance of the action of the tides in the Channel. With calm eventually restored, he divided the whole of Gaul into several provinces; and the subsequent mingling of the indigenous Celtic population with Roman troops and traders and their families—an association which continued for over five hundred years—was the foundation of modern French culture.

The End of the First Triumvirate: 49 BC

Halfway through his Gallic campaign, Caesar had to return briefly to Italy to meet with Crassus and Pompey to try to ease the strains in their relationship; each of them had some anxiety about the personal ambitions of the others, and plans for the future had to be agreed upon. It was decided that Caesar's command in Gaul should be extended for another five years and that Pompey and Crassus should be consuls for 55. In the following year the Senate appointed Pompey governor of Spain, but he arranged to serve *in absentia*: thus he had command of the Roman troops posted there, just in case, and at the same time he did not have to be away from the action in Rome. Crassus meanwhile received his own military command, a glamorous proconsulship in Syria where he could make war on the Parthians. But at the battle of Carrhae in 53, he was soundly defeated, his standards were captured and he himself was killed. In the previous year, Julia (Caesar's daughter) had died in childbirth, and the sentimental tie between the two remaining triumvirs was broken. From that moment both of them schemed to bring about the downfall of the other: obviously Rome was not big enough for both of them.

In 53, rioting broke out in Rome between the supporters of Pompey and Caesar. The Senate began to panic at the thought of Caesar's return—they had no idea what he might have in mind—and they put Pompey into office as sole consul. They then accused Caesar of crimes against the state, alleging that during his consul-

ship of 59 he had used force to put into law the demands of the triumvirate, and that he had illegally extended his provincial command. Pompey could not join in the attack, both because he had condoned what Caesar had done and because his own position as absentee governor of Spain would certainly not bear scrutiny. He did not know what to do, and so he did nothing.

Caesar in his province also faced a dilemma. If he returned to Rome alone, there would be nothing to prevent his being tried and found guilty by the Senate—and that would mean the end of his career. But if he brought his troops with him, he would be breaking the law of Sulla which forbade a general to lead his army outside the boundaries of his province without permission—and so he would in effect be declaring civil war. Though neither he nor Pompey wanted war, neither was willing to make concessions to the other. After they had both made various unsuccessful proposals for mutual disarmament, and with negotiations at a stalemate, the Senate passed the same emergency *consultum ultimum* as they had against Gaius Gracchus, and instructed Pompey to take up arms against Caesar if Caesar would not disarm unilaterally. For three days in the spring of 49 Caesar hesitated while he kept his thoughts to himself:

> He went to the theatre, inspected the site of a proposed school for gladiators and gave a dinner party, all in order to ally suspicion that anything unusual was afoot. But after dark he requisitioned a pair of mules and a cart... and set off with his lieutenants towards the frontier. Their lights blew out and they became hopelessly lost... but at dawn they met a peasant who took them on foot through the back lanes until he could once more set them on their right road. Caesar came up to his troops on the banks of the Rubicon, the river that marked the boundary between Cisalpine Gaul and Italy...
>
> He stood, still hesitating, on the bank; and then he saw a human figure, larger than life and eerily beautiful, playing on a reed pipe and surrounded by a group of shepherds and some of Caesar's soldiers who had drift-

ed away from their formation. Suddenly the figure snatched a trumpet from a soldier, blew a call and moved across the river. "It is a sign from the gods," said Caesar. "Let us follow his lead, and take vengeance on those who have betrayed us."

(Suetonius: *Lives of the Twelve Caesars, Julius Caesar* 31)

So his mind was made up. "*Alea iacta est* (The die is cast)," he said, and entered Italy at the head of his legions.

Infantrymen at ease before going on duty, with the *aquila* in the background. (Art Resource)

12. Julius Caesar

The Civil War between Pompey and Caesar: 49 – 46 BC

Pompey had hoped that the population of Italy would spontaneously rise up to oppose Caesar and his approaching army. But when this did not happen, Pompey determined that there should be no battles in Italy, as there had been between Marius and Sulla, and that any real fighting should take place abroad. With the consuls and all the Senate, he evacuated Rome and sailed for Greece from Brundisium. There, with an army collected from the province of Syria, he awaited Caesar's pursuit. Caesar followed him at the head of his own loyal army, and at Pharsalus he decisively defeated Pompey's forces. Looking at the dead bodies— mostly senators and nobles—Caesar is said to have commented sadly, "*Hoc voluerunt* (This is what they wanted)." He realized that he had been forced into the war against his will, and his victory was not a triumph but a tragedy.

Pompey fled to Egypt. As he came ashore in Alexandria, he was stabbed by agents of the fifteen-year-old king Ptolemy XIII, who thought that he was doing Caesar a favor. Pompey's head and signet ring were sent to Caesar, who wept when he saw them; he and Pompey had once been friends, and he had never expected their political feud to end like this.

Egypt at this time was involved in its own civil war between factions in support of Ptolemy and of his co-regent, his elder sister Cleopatra. As was the custom in the Egyptian royal family, they were married to each other, even though Egypt was a Hellenistic monarchy; the Ptolemies were Macedonians, direct descendants of one of Alexander's generals, and therefore imbued with Greek rather than African ideals. Caesar's troops were drawn into the fighting, interrupted only by an expedition to put down a rebellion in Asia Minor. Caesar, always famous for his speed of action, dealt with the rebels in one swift engagement: "*Veni vidi vici* (I came, I saw, I conquered)," he said. Ptolemy was deposed and killed. Other casualties were the great library at Alexandria, which was accidentally set on fire, and Caesar's heart, which he lost to Cleopatra. She soon became his mistress, and when the war ended he set her up in style in Rome, much to the disapproval of the Romans, who—whatever their private predilections—were prudes where their leaders were concerned.

The Dictatorship of Julius Caesar: 46 – 44 BC

In 46, Caesar returned to Italy. What was left of the Senate welcomed him and at once appointed him dictator, like Sulla in 82, with a mandate to restore order in the state. Unlike Sulla, however, Caesar did not execute or exile any remaining supporters of Pompey's, thus giving notice that he had no specific axes of his own to grind except insofar as to make the existing system more effective. He enlarged the Senate to nine hundred, first replacing the members who had been killed during the civil war, and then including enough Italians to make it truly representative of the state as a whole. He took away the Senate's responsibility for finance and foreign policy and the disposition of provincial commands, and reserved those rights for himself; he manipulated the elections in order to get the magistrates he wanted, and in particular he made sure that he himself was annually elected as one of the two consuls, even while he remained dictator. Finally, he assured himself of the loyalty of the army by awarding it a substantial pay increase. There were to be no opportunities for rivals.

In an extensive program of public works, paid for by new taxes, he paved roads and opened another forum. He drained a large area of marshland outside the city to provide more farmland, and began the construction of another Senate House to replace the one which had been burnt down in previous rioting. Many residents of the provinces were made Roman citizens, including all the men in his favorite legion, "the Lark," which he had recruited in Gaul. By establishing Roman colonies overseas to provide land for his own veterans and for some of the urban poor, he ensured the spread of Roman ideas all around the Mediterranean and the Middle East.

One of Caesar's most important changes was his reform of the old Etruscan calendar, which was still in use. This system had gone badly out of synchronization with the progress of the lunar months, and attempts to correct it during the early republic by adding two extra months (January and February) at the start of the year had not been sufficient. Caesar borrowed most of his new calendar from the Egyptians, adding extra days to some months and introducing leap years; finally, in a self-congratulatory moment, he renamed the seventh month Julius. With only a few minor changes made by Pope Gregory XIII in 1582, Caesar's calendar is still in use in the West today.

The Assassination of Julius Caesar: 44 BC

Caesar's reforms could hardly be criticized because they were not useful or because they did not work; but there was considerable anxiety regarding Caesar's own role in the government. For all those who admired him for what he had achieved, there were others who felt he had moved too fast, and without proper respect for people's feelings or the traditions of Rome. In truth, Caesar often seemed cold and distant; he had no patience for non-cooperation, and did not suffer fools gladly. He was arrogant—and arrogance can often be mistaken for ambition. In the Senate especially, though members for the sake of peace and quiet had acquiesced to Caesar's abrupt removal of their responsibilities, many did not believe that their acquiescence should signal perpetual subservience to him. And as they heard what Caesar said with his lips, they began to wonder what he intended in his heart, and whether he was not ignoring what was right for the sake of what was expedient.

Increasingly conservative republicans began to ask the old question, as they had asked it in the past about Gaius Gracchus, Sulla and Pompey: did Caesar mean to make himself king? Had he not allowed his portrait to appear on coins, unprecedented in anyone's own lifetime; and had not his statue been put up along-side those of the seven original kings? And had he not encouraged the founding of a religious cult around himself, in imitation of the practice of the Hellenistic kingdoms? Why did he sometimes appear in a purple robe? And what about the rumor that Cleopatra wanted to be queen of Rome as well as Egypt? And that offer of a crown at a public festival—to be sure he had pushed it away, but with how much reluctance? Certainly, like Sulla, Caesar saw the Senate as out-of-date and reactionary, incapable of dealing with the complexities of governing an empire. And certainly he had stated that Sulla had been foolish in voluntarily resigning his dictatorship. But equally certainly Caesar was visibly annoyed at any reference to monarchy: "*Non sum rex,*" he would grumble, "*sed Caesar* (I am Caesar, not a king)."

But for a few senators, led by Gaius Cassius and Marcus Brutus—who could not forget that he was descended from that Brutus who had been one of the first two consuls when Tarquin the Proud was expelled in 509—the time for asking questions was over. They had whispered conversations in public places, they held agitated meetings in private houses, and at last their minds were made up: Caesar must go.

If Caesar had any wind of the plot, he would not admit to fear, and he told his friends that in fact he would prefer a quick and unexpected death. He refused a bodyguard, he refused to change any of his daily routines, and he refused to take any notice of warnings or omens.

> *Apart from shooting stars, noises in the night, and wild birds which settled on the buildings in the Forum—events that might normally not be thought to give information about the fate of important personages—there was an apparition of warriors fighting with each other in the clouds and glowing with an incandescent light. A soldier had his hand burst into flames, although afterwards—contrary to all expectations—there was no trace of any injury. An animal that was being sacrificed by*

Caesar was found to be missing its heart—a very bad sign indeed, because without a heart nothing can stay alive. It was also widely rumored that Caesar had been warned of a great danger that would threaten him on the Ides of March, and on that very day, on his way to a meeting of the Senate, he had met the man who had warned him. "The Ides of March have come," said Caesar, jokingly. But the man had answered him with great seriousness: "Yes, they have come, but not gone."

(Plutarch: *Life of Julius Caesar* 63)

It was, then, on the Ides (15th) of March of 44, that Caesar went to preside at a meeting of the Senate in the theater built by his rival Pompey—his own new Senate House was not yet complete. In the middle of the morning's business, he was surrounded by twenty-three conspirators and stabbed twenty-three times. As he fell, he looked straight into Brutus' eyes and reproached him—for Brutus, despite all their differences was an old friend. His blood splashed up over the statue of Pompey. He was dead.

13. The Second Triumvirate: 43 BC

Mark Antony takes Charge *Cicero*

It is doubtful whether anyone seriously considered that Caesar's death would lead to a restoration to the old republic. Even Cicero, who had never had anything good to say about Caesar, said that Brutus and Cassius had acted "with the courage of men but the forethought of children." The Senate proposed no one to take Caesar's place, and Marcus Antonius (Mark Antony) who had been Caesar's colleague in the consulship of 44, acted with great energy and dispatch to enter the vacuum and to bolster his own position as Caesar's successor.

To calm the apprehension of Caesar's supporters among the people, Antony sensibly announced that all Caesar's laws and reforms would remain in force. Equally sensibly, he soothed the republicans by abolishing the office of dictator, and granting amnesty to the conspirators. But he could not allow Caesar's death to appear to go unavenged. He therefore summoned the people to the forum, where by parading Caesar's body and by reading Caesar's will—according to which, he claimed, a small sum of money was left to every Roman citizen—he provoked a riot against the conspirators so that they fled the city. At the same time Antony made sure that he himself did not lose the conspirators' favor. He arranged with the Senate that Brutus and Cassius should be given proconsulships in the East; they left Rome, and in their provinces began to raise armies who would be loyal to them.

The Arrival of Octavian

It is not clear whether Antony had forged that part of Caesar's will that he had read to the people, but he could not alter the reality of Caesar's heir and adopted son—his grand-nephew Octavianus (usually known as Octavian), now an eighteen-year-old university student in Greece. As soon as he learned of

Caesar's death, Octavian had come immediately to Rome; and his first move was to pay a courtesy visit to Cicero. Although he did not fully trust him, Cicero was impressed and flattered by Octavian's attentions; and he advised the Senate to give its full support to Octavian if only to get rid of Antony, who he had by now decided was entirely unscrupulous—another Caesar, only worse. He then made a series of speeches—now called the *Philippics*, after Demosthenes' famous tirades against Philip II of Macedonia—in which he attacked Antony with ever-increasing violence.

> *Your acts against the law at least showed some kind of energy. But enough of them—let me speak now of your acts of trivial thoughtlessness. At Hippias' wedding you succeeded in drinking so much—sucking the stuff down your throat with your gladiator's lungs and muscles— that the next day you threw up in full view of the Roman people. It was not only disgusting to see it then, it is disgusting even to hear about it now. Bad enough if it had happened at a private party, after you had been chugging from one of those enormous mugs of yours. But you were... on official business before the assembly of the Roman people. When even a hiccup would have been out of place, you vomited up chunks of food still stinking of wine, first into your lap and then all over the speaker's platform...*
>
> *However, you have made your own bed. Now I shall speak for myself. When I was a young man I fought for the republic; I will not desert her now that I am old. If I thought nothing of Catiline's sword, shall I be scared by yours? I would be glad to give up my life, if by my death freedom could be restored to my country.*

(Cicero: *Philippic* ii. 25, 45)

Meanwhile Antony was finding it impossible to pin Octavian down. Octavian, though very young and very skinny, was a good deal tougher than he looked. He and Antony argued about Caesar's money—Antony seems to have embezzled some fairly considerable sums—and about each other's political standing. Octavian raised an army from among Caesar's old soldiers, and Antony accused Octavian of planning to assassinate him. Fighting broke out. Antony withdrew to the north and joined forces with an old lieutenant of Caesar's, Lepidus, who was now governor of one of the provinces of Transalpine Gaul. The Senate, simultaneously encouraged by Cicero, alarmed at the prospect of civil war breaking out all over again, and wary of Octavian's troops, appointed Octavian consul for 43 (though he was not yet twenty). Then they instructed a tribune to propose in the assembly a law (the *lex Titia*) that would put Lepidus, Antony and Octavian in joint control of the state. The law was passed, and the association later known as the Second Triumvirate came legally into existence.

The Second Triumvirate: 43 - 42 BC

The second Triumvirate was very different from the first, which had been an entirely unofficial group who wanted to put persuasive pressure on the Senate. The second was formally created by the Senate and People of Rome, who had handed over to three individuals unlimited powers in war and peace, at home and abroad. This implied that they had given up all their own rights, and in effect put the Roman republic out of existence.

The first act of this new dictatorship—even though it was never so called—was to follow the example of Sulla by drawing up proscription lists to get rid of its enemies. The most famous victim was Cicero, for Antony had not forgotten the *Philippics*. It was a sad irony that Cicero, the republic's greatest champion of moderation and conciliation, should meet his death by despotic violence. But the proscriptions damaged Octavian too: history has not forgiven him for his part in these pointless murders. Though he may genuinely have wished to avenge Caesar, Octavian might have remembered that Caesar was famous for his clemency.

Having made it clear that they would tolerate no opposition, the triumvirs now began to nominate magistrates to serve both in Italy and in the provinces, and then to raise an army that would deal with Caesar's assassins. Leaving Lepidus behind in case of trouble at home, Octavian and Antony crossed into Greece, where they defeated the armies of Brutus and Cassius in two engagements at Philippi. These victories left dead the last of the aristocrats who might have offered serious resistance to Octavian or Antony. Brutus and Cassius committed suicide in the old-fashioned Roman way, by running onto swords held by their slaves.

After the battles of Philippi, the triumvirate broke up. Lepidus, who could not make up his mind whether to be ambitious or phlegmatic, was packed off into early retirement; Antony stayed in the East to guard the borders of the provinces, and Octavian returned to Rome.

Octavian and Agrippa

Comets and other auspicious omens welcomed Octavian, and the poet Vergil wrote an ode in which he forecast the arrival of a mysterious child who would rule over a new Golden Age. Yet the immediate reality was harsh. Octavian was still regarded with some suspicion as a newcomer to the political scene, and many Romans preferred Antony's more cheerful down-to-earth manner. Despite Caesar's building projects, much of Italy was run-down or neglected; in Rome there were food riots, and in the countryside unpopular confiscations of land in order to settle the veterans; and Pompey's son, Sextus, calling himself a second Neptune, had raised an armed revolt in Sicily.

To restore order would have been a daunting job even for an experienced administrator, but Octavian was still in his early twenties; and it took him ten years of pushing and pulling, of threats and promises, to succeed. He was buoyed through these difficult years by the faithful service of Marcus Agrippa, who became his closest friend and ally. Agrippa's energy in the campaign at sea against Sextus Pompeius, whom he defeated in 36, made up for Octavian's lack of military experience; and as aedile he was able to boost Octavian's popularity by undertaking an ambitious program of urban reconstruction, by cleaning up the water supply and by lengthening the list of those who were eligible for the distribution of cheap wheat.

Antony and Cleopatra

While Octavian was busy in Italy, Antony, who liked soldiering much more than politics, was enjoying himself on the far frontiers of the empire. He subdued the northern tribes who threatened Macedonia; in Syria he rolled back an invasion by the Parthians; and he created a new client-kingdom in Armenia which would protect the eastern borders. But military campaigns cost money, and to beg, borrow or steal it, Antony decided to go to Egypt, where Cleopatra, having been ignominiously smuggled out of Rome after the assassination of Caesar, was back on the throne.

Antony had met Cleopatra before, when he was serving in Egypt with Caesar during the civil war, and he remembered her well. Captivated exactly like Caesar, he now became her lover. Cleopatra, however, was clever—fully as clever as Antony—and she ruthlessly used her feminine wiles to get fair return for the money that she decided to give him.

Plato says that there are four kinds of flattery, but Cleopatra had mastered a thousand. It made no difference whether Antony was in a silly or serious mood: she always had some delightful trick to capture his attention. She was always with him, and she did not let him out of her sight by day or night. She played dice with him, she drank with him, she went hunting with him; she would go into the field to watch him when he was on military exercises...

One day Antony was fishing with Cleopatra, and while she was there he had no luck. So he quietly ordered a fisherman to dive down and hook onto the end of his line some fish which had already been caught. When he pulled in his "catch," Cleopatra spotted what was going on, but she pretended to be overcome with admiration and proudly announced to everyone what a great angler Antony was. "You must come to see him," she said. So a crowd assembled on Antony's boat; but one of Cleopatra's slaves got at his hook before Antony's man could, and fastened onto it a fish from Bithynia, already cooked and salted. He made his cast, felt a movement on the line and hauled it in. When they saw what he had snagged, everyone roared with laughter, and Cleopatra said to him: "Fishing is a sport better left to the monarchs of poor old Egypt—you had better stick to catching cities and provinces and kingdoms."

(Plutarch: *Life of Mark Antony* 29)

So Antony was trapped. He promised on his own initiative to cede large parts of Roman provinces to Cleopatra, to her son by Caesar, Cesarion, and to their own twin children, to whom they had given the splendid names of Alexander the Sun and Cleopatra the Moon. The news of these "Alexandrian donations" caused a sensation in Rome as well as among Antony's own troops, but the besotted Antony, like Caesar before him, had apparently given no thought to the offense that his alliance with the Egyptian queen would cause.

Octavian's family honor was also insulted because Antony was married to his sister, and public anger over the arbitrary distribution of Roman territory made it easy for him to rally support against Antony. In 32, the whole population of Italy took an oath of allegiance—perhaps voluntarily, perhaps not—to Octavian, and this show of support gave him the confidence and the mandate to declare war. The enemy technically was Cleopatra, though of course he really wanted to be rid of Antony.

Hostilities were quick and almost anticlimactic. Antony, with Cleopatra at this side, advanced into Greece, and Octavian's forces came to meet him. In a preliminary maneuver, Agrippa tried to tempt Antony and Cleopatra into a naval engagement off the cape of Actium on the west coast of Greece. Vergil—with a certain amount of poetic license—describes the scene:

> *The white spray and blue water of the ocean shimmered... and dolphins jumped and dived and flicked their tails... From his high poop deck [Octavian] commanded the forces of the Senate and people of Rome, and all the Roman gods watched over him. Flames of good omen flickered round his temples and his father's star shone above him; and his lieutenant, the tireless Agrippa, wore a wreath that he had been awarded for his naval victories in the past—the gods always sent him the weather that he needed.*
>
> *Opposite them: Mark Antony. His ships were all barbarian opulence, and his crews were drawn from all the nations he had subdued. They came from the countries that lie nearest to the dawn, from Egypt, from the coast of the Red Sea, from Bactria and Asia. And the queen of Egypt, Cleopatra—that name should not be spoken aloud—followed him. From the shelter of the shore the fleets approached each other at speed. Spray flew. Oars dipped and swung. Bows sliced the boiling sea apart. On forecastles and poops, men were so thickly clustered that you might have thought that every island of the Aegean had been uprooted and was on the move; or that you were witnessing the collision of mountains.*

(Vergil: *Aeneid* viii. 671)

In fact, as soon as Agrippa's fleet came into view, Cleopatra's ships turned and fled unceremoniously back to Egypt. Without them, Antony's ships were greatly outnumbered, and he followed without a backward glance. Octavian unhurriedly made his way to Egypt and occupied Alexandria, and Antony and Cleopatra both committed suicide in order to avoid the humiliation of capture. He stabbed himself, and she smuggled a viper into the tower where

Roman forces had her penned up, and let it bite her. Octavian spared the lives of most of Antony's soldiers, but he had Cesarion murdered. Then he cancelled the Alexandrian donations, confiscated the Egyptian treasury to pay his own troops, and annexed Egypt as a special province in his own personal possession. A hundred years of civil war were over, and he returned in triumph to Rome.

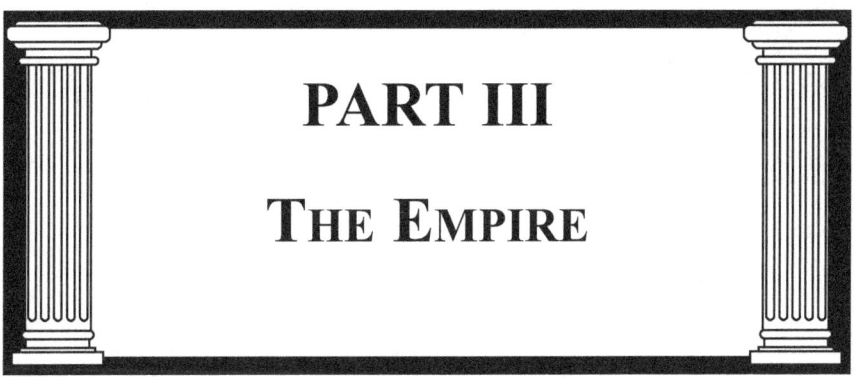

PART III

THE EMPIRE

14. The Principate of Augustus

What's in a Name?

With the passing of the *lex Titia*, by which the Second Triumvirate was formed in 43, the Roman republican constitution, and the democratic freedoms of the people, had officially come to an end. In 31, with the battle of Actium behind him and his last rival off the stage, Octavian emerged, alone and unopposed, as the absolute ruler of an entirely new and fundamentally different Rome. The collection of provinces governed by elected Roman magistrates had long been loosely called an empire, but from now on it would be ruled by an emperor, and in its reconstituted form would be known to historians as "the Roman Empire."

However, the Latin word *imperator*, from which *emperor* is derived, had specifically military connotations. Octavian's primary aim was to establish a lasting peace, and he always chose to refer to himself instead as *Princeps*. He intended this word to imply that he was no more than first citizen, or first among equals; it also happened to be the title of the senior member of the Senate, and so had a comfortable old-fashioned ring. He was also addressed by the familiar cognomen inherited through his great uncle's family, Caesar. This name would later become the generic title for all subsequent emperors, whether or not they were

Augustus as a young man. (Photograph © 2004 Museum of Fine Arts, Boston)

related to Octavian, and from it are derived the German *Kaiser* and the Russian *Czar*. In 27, the Senate flattered Octavian by giving him his own cognomen, Augustus—and from then on this was the name by which he was always known. In Latin *augustus* meant "revered," but the word also had a religious significance because of its etymological connection with the Etruscan *auguria* (the art of interpreting omens from the gods), and so it came to suggest that the gods had determined the nature of the emperor's new role. Four years later, the Senate flattered Augustus further by naming the eighth month after him and awarding him the most prestigious title of all—*Pater Patriae*: the father of the country.

Organization and Administration

In a memoir published at the end of his life, Augustus wrote:

After I had brought to an end all the civil wars, and gained complete control, and won universal support, I transferred the power to make all decisions concerning the republic out of my own hands and back to the Senate and people of Rome. And for this action the Senate decreed that I should be called Augustus, that the doorposts of my house should be wreathed with laurel, and that a garland should be fixed over my door... After this time I was superior to everyone else in my authority, but I had in fact no more power than those others who were my colleagues in the magistracies.

Though—with the approval of the Senate and people of Rome,—I was appointed guardian of public laws and morals, to act by myself and with supreme power, I accepted no office unless it was consistent with the customs of our ancestors.

(Augustus: *Res Gestae* 2. 34)

If there were those who did not agree with this self-assessment, or with the appeal to the *mos maiorum*, they took care not to complain in public:

Gradually Augustus swept aside all opposition, taking to himself the functions of the Senate, the magistrates, and the lawgivers. Anyone who had any spirit of independence in him was dead, as the result either of war or execution. Those who were left behind found out that if they did exactly as they were told, they would do well in politics or business. They had already done well out of the civil wars, and for them it was better to be safe under the new arrangements than sorry under the old ones.

(Tacitus: *Annals* i.2)

Had Augustus indeed restored the old republic? Had he in any sense transferred the power back to the Senate and people? Outwardly all the old institutions and offices remained in place. The Senate was not disbanded; but it chose not to take advantage even of the opportunities that Augustus offered it, and instead turned its discussions with him into silent acts of obedience. The frank and impassioned speeches that for so long had been a mark of senatorial debate were no longer admired, and the Roman tradition of oratory began to die out. Only the courts of law remained under the Senate's control, but even there appeals could be made directly to the emperor.

Every year, as before, the people's assembly elected magistrates: but the difference now was that the emperor was always elected as one of the consuls—with a colleague who would defer to him on all occasions. In 23, the Senate voted Augustus permanent proconsular *imperium* and permanent *tribunicia potestas* (the power of the tribune). This was crucial: as tribune, Augustus could convene the Senate and also propose legislation—always of course under the safe assumption that it would be approved and passed. And as a last resort he had the tribune's veto. But beyond any constitutional office, he possessed—as he himself admitted— the force of his personality: his expectation that he would be obeyed without question, his personal *auctoritas* (authority or prestige), derived not from law but from respect.

There was left, then, the question as to who should be responsible for the administration of the Empire. When Augustus decided that he must institute a professional civil service, he turned not to the Senate—even stripped of power, its members still would not deign to work for pay—but rather to the *equites*, and he used freed slaves to perform most of the clerical work. Equites were also appointed to serve as the emperor's deputies in his own province of Egypt, and to supervise the grain supply from Egypt, Africa and Asia. Equites commanded the fleets and the praetorian guard (the emperor's bodyguard); and they also took charge of Rome's first firefighters—a force of six hundred slaves (later freedmen) who would form a bucket brigade to bring water from the Tiber to the site of the fire—and of its first police force, which helped to deter riots, but could do little to prevent endemic crime in the streets.

In all this the role of the people's assembly was entirely diminished: the emperor pre-arranged the elections and any votes on legislation were no more than formal gestures. But Augustus might have argued that the people did not deserve a role. For nearly two hundred years now, they had ceased to be the cool-headed partners of the Senate, willing to listen to reason and rational debate. They had gradually lost such power as the constitution had given them and had become the instruments first of well-meaning reformers like the Gracchi and later of unprincipled rabble-rousers. In any case they showed no sign of wanting their freedom back. While the equites were fully occupied in the civil service bureaucracy or with their profitable business connections, the middle classes were content to enjoy the peace that Augustus had brought them, in which they could make an uninterrupted living from their market stalls, their workshops or their farms, and the urban *proletarii* accepted poverty and unemployment as long as they had their *panem et circenses* (bread and circuses).

Provincial and Foreign Policy

The single most important lesson which Augustus had

learned from the civil wars was that independent action by ambitious generals operating out of their provinces must be forestalled. Marius, Sulla, Pompey and Caesar all had secured political power by using, or threatening to use, their armies in order to put pressure on the Senate. Augustus therefore divided the provinces into two groups: an outer "imperial" ring which was to be governed by himself, with equites as his financial officers; and an inner "senatorial" ring, governed in the traditional way by pro-magistrates appointed by the Senate. Armies were to be stationed only in the imperial provinces, under the emperor's direct control and commanded by generals whom he appointed personally. These troops were to be paid from the treasury rather than by the emperor himself, with money raised from death duties and a sales tax.

As they did with all their other prerogatives, the senators silently ceded to Augustus their right to make foreign policy. And Augustus' policy was a simple one: to keep the Empire within its existing borders, and to annex new territory only to straighten them or to push them out to natural boundaries provided by rivers or mountain ranges.

In the north, a border war was fought against some of the German tribes, directed by the emperor's stepsons Tiberius and Drusus; and in a disaster which haunted Augustus ever afterwards, the Germans ambushed a Roman general in the deep forests and captured his standards. But in Parthia there was more success: a Roman army recovered the standards which had been lost by Crassus at the battle of Carrhae, and a peace treaty was signed which allowed Roman merchants to pass through Parthia to India and China, where they traded for silk. Throughout the East the religious cult of *Augustus et Roma* was encouraged in order to satisfy the local peoples accustomed to worship their kings as gods; in return many Eastern cults (such as the worship of the Egyptian Isis) were introduced to Rome by soldiers returning from abroad.

There was much unrest in Syria, and also to the south in Judaea—a client kingdom ruled by king Herod until his death in AD 6 and then a province. Despite the anti-Roman sentiment stirred up by the Jews, Augustus extended to them the Romans' habitual religious toleration: Jews were exempted from military service and no portrait of the emperor was allowed to appear on their coins, in deference to Moses' prohibition of "graven images."

In Judaea there also occurred a significant incident, which went quite unnoticed at the time. Just before Herod's death, Augustus required that a census be taken throughout all the provinces, and in Judaea, for the purpose of assessing taxes more fairly. In the village of Bethlehem, more people had gathered to be counted than could find lodging for the night. In a makeshift shelter, a woman went into labor, and she named her child Jesus.

Public Morality in the Principate

For the sake of the efficiency of the administration and the security of the Empire, every possible contingency had apparently been provided for; but Augustus had not foreseen the decline in public morals that would come about when all the tasks of government were concentrated in the emperor's hands. With few official duties or responsibilities, many of the senatorial class now gave themselves over to acquiring the luxuries that were offered by increased foreign trade and overseas contacts.

So the infamous vices of the Romans were in fact almost entirely the vices of the aristocrats. Though they were not necessarily the only ones who could afford the orgies, the banquets lavish to the point of obscenity, or the dancing girls, they were the only ones who had the leisure to enjoy them. But even the nobles' wealth was not inexhaustible. Though they wanted ever more expensive pleasures, at the same time they did not wish to sell off their land or their mansions in order to pay for them; consequently corruption and usury flourished. Their crimes and excesses were a frequent topic for contemporary historians and satirists, who took a high moral tone but were never able to resist a scandal.

The trends that had begun to undermine family life after the

Punic wars continued: more celibacy, more divorce, and more remarriages. Marriage, particularly among the rich, had become little more than a convention to produce an heir; and it often served as an instrument to pursue politics by other means, to join together influential families or individuals. It was, for example, for political reasons that Pompey had married Caesar's daughter, and Antony had married Octavia; Augustus made his daughter Julia marry three different men, one after the other, to further his own policies. And not surprisingly, the emperor's attempts to legislate morality were futile. Sumptuary laws against excessive spending, laws against adultery, tax breaks for married men—none of this legislation had any effect on a growing trend toward self-indulgence. Society had become obsessed with gossip, entertainment and sports; it was only a few intellectuals who were not caught up in the fervor of the games:

> *I spent a most delightful quiet day, reading and writing. I hear you saying, "But you were in the city—what a way to occupy your time!" Well, there were games that day—and the games are a spectacle that does not interest me in the slightest. There's nothing new, nothing different, nothing which would be worth seeing even once. I am amazed that so many thousands of adults can behave so much like children—just watching horses running about and men standing in chariots behind them.*
>
> *If they were interested in the form of the horses or the skill of the drivers, I suppose I could understand it. But they support one team or another only because of the team's colors, and that's what they get so worked up about. If, in the course of a race, one team's colors were to be switched with another's, the crowd's enthusiasm and support would be switched too, and they wouldn't take a second look at the drivers and horses that just a few minutes before they had been cheering on.*
>
> (Pliny the Younger: *Letters* ix)

The Problem of the Emperor's Successor

Many Romans must have wished—or even believed—that Augustus would live forever, but he knew well that he was only a mortal, and fairly early in his principate he began to plan for his successor. Augustus' personal pride, as well as the long established republican tradition that sons should follow their fathers into public service, suggested that the next *princeps* should come from within his own family. He therefore decided that, as soon as a candidate had proved his energy and competence, he should be clearly designated, and then, at the appropriate moment, the Senate could go through a formal process of confirming and electing him into office. It was a sensible policy, and it was not Augustus' fault that it did not work out as well as he had hoped.

From his first marriage, Augustus had only a daughter, Julia; and he had no children with his second wife, Livia. But he did have a nephew Marcellus—the son of his sister Octavia—whose early public appearances had made him popular with the Roman people. Augustus' eye, then, fell first on him; and he was duly married off to his young cousin Julia. But when, having shown nothing but promise, Marcellus died of a fever (probably malaria) in 21, Augustus turned to his old friend Agrippa.

Agrippa had felt from the start that he should have been considered, and had been openly jealous of Marcellus. But now Augustus smoothed his feathers by giving him tribunician power at home and the command of the eastern imperial provinces, so that he should have experience in all aspects of the principate if the worst should happen. He was then brought into the emperor's family by two routes: Augustus officially adopted him as his son, and also had him marry Julia, though she had barely recovered from the shock of Marcellus' death. The marriage presented certain difficulties: Julia was only eighteen and Agrippa was forty-two; and the two of them had quite different personalities. When Julia began to run with wild friends of her own age, Agrippa was deeply embarrassed. But in 12 BC he died, leaving Julia with no less than five children from their seven years of unhappy marriage, of which the two eldest were the boys Lucius and Gaius. Augustus was delighted with his grandsons, who grew into bright and engaging teenagers, and either of them, he thought, would do very well as his heir. He began their training by making them consuls as soon as they reached the age of twenty, and then sending them off to serve in the provinces. But Marcellus' bad luck followed them: they both died abroad, one of fever in AD 2 and the other of wounds in AD 4.

There was now left only Augustus' stepson Tiberius, who was Livia's son by her previous marriage. Tiberius was by now in his late forties, and as a young man he had been happily married to

Cameo with Livia and Tiberius. (Photograph © 2004 Museum of Fine Arts, Boston)

Agrippa's daughter Vipsania. But after Agrippa's death, Augustus had forced him to divorce Vipsania and marry poor Julia, who had long been his stepsister and was now his stepmother-in-law as well. Tiberius hated Julia, and Julia herself became so demoralized by this third marriage of convenience that her private behavior turned into a public scandal. As punishment, Augustus banished her to a tiny island off Naples, and gave instructions that he never again wished to hear her name mentioned in his presence.

Tiberius was sour and disillusioned, and no wonder. He had loved his first wife, but she had been taken away from him; his second wife had disgraced him; he had enjoyed his career in the army, but he had no desire at all to be the next emperor, especially since he was so obviously Augustus' last choice. Nevertheless at Gaius' death he was given the tribunician power and proconsular *imperium*; and for the next ten years he was in effect co-emperor with Augustus. Like Agrippa before him, he was formally adopted as Augustus' son.

Only Livia seemed completely pleased. The gossip in Rome was that she had plotted for Tiberius' succession all along, and that the death of all the previously designated heirs had not necessarily been natural or even accidental.

15. Art for Art's Sake?

Art and Politics

Augustus' principate was more than a triumph of organization and administration. Despite criticism that he had substituted despotism for democracy—flawed though the democracy had been—Augustus gave a free hand to artists and writers, commissioning many projects himself. His encouragement of the arts was not, of course, entirely altruistic: Augustus was a master of propaganda, and many—some would suggest most—of the works of his principate were deliberately conceived to glorify the emperor's position and his achievements. Art and politics were particularly well co-ordinated under the patronage of Maecenas, Augustus' closest friend and advisor after Agrippa. Although he never held office, Maecenas counseled the emperor constantly on policy as well as keeping him informed of useful new talent. He was extremely influential in his own support of new writers and artists: he was rich enough to subsidize them financially and, by buying their work, to set trends and fashions.

Art and Architecture

The Romans' art, like everything else in their culture, was a construction of other people's ideas, modified by their own requirements. As might be expected then, Roman sculptors were enormously influenced by the Greeks. The richest Romans collected original Greek frescoes and sculpture for their private houses, especially that of the fifth and fourth centuries BC, either buying it or simply appropriating it, like the infamous Verres, the corrupt governor of Sicily who had been prosecuted by Cicero in a sensational trial. But a far larger number, who could not find or afford originals, were happy to possess reproductions, and an entire statue-copying industry grew up in Rome. Though many of the Greek originals have been lost, accurate and successful copies have frequently survived, even though it is possible for an expert to tell one from the other by examining the details of their technique.

The chief characteristic of classical Greek sculpture was its idealism; the Greeks represented the human figure, for instance, as they thought it should be rather than as it was. However, Roman artists were also interested in realistic portraits. Portraits that have survived on coins and busts show us what many famous figures of Roman history really looked like, warts and all. But when Roman realism and Greek idealism were combined in a single work, the effect was not happy: it is disconcerting to see the head of a venerable, wrinkled statesman attached to the perfectly muscled young body of an athlete.

The wealthier Romans copied the Greeks in the design of their private houses: the rooms opened off an ornate central courtyard (*atrium*) often with a fish-pool in the middle, but presented a blank facade to the street. Hot air was passed through terra-cotta pipes below the floor, and the rooms were decorated in the Etruscan fashion with frescoes of landscapes and mythological scenes.

Roman theatres were recognizably copied from Greek originals, but there was always a tendency to construct more elaborate permanent backdrops, and to push the stage further forward into what had traditionally been the circular space of the orchestra. In their temples, too, the Romans usually followed the standard Greek model, though frequently with the addition of extra stories below and above. They often varied the exterior with a colonnade of Corinthian columns, which the Greeks had used only for interior ornamentation. But in other buildings, the Romans improved on the Greek and Egyptian *pylon*—two columns and a lintel, shaped like the letter *pi*—as a method of spanning a space. The arch, though originally an Etruscan invention, was modified over many years and turned out to be much stronger and more versatile than the pylon. The Romans took the arch and used it in various new combinations that were peculiarly their own. They spanned valleys with aqueducts and viaducts; and they developed the dome and the barrel vault, which is called a *basilica* when it appears in a large building such as a law court, a shopping arcade or a temple.

At the end of his life, Augustus boasted that he had "found Rome built of brick and left it of marble." In an ambitious program of public works, his motive was doubtless the same as that of Pericles when he rebuilt the temples on the Acropolis of Athens. Not only did the glittering new temples, baths and theaters provide construction and maintenance jobs for the poor, but they also doubtless inspired an appropriate sense of awe and civic pride among the Romans as well as visitors from the provinces or foreign countries.

Yet behind the ostentatious mask of public buildings the city

Modern reconstruction of the Altar of Peace, dedicated by a grateful Senate to Augustus in 9 BC. (Art Resource)

had another face. Its most characteristic feature was the blocks of tenement houses, called *insulae* (islands), where most people lived in comparative squalor. The insulae were several stories high, because it was cheaper to build upwards than sideways in the limited space available. Usually consisting of shops on the ground floor and apartments above, they were poorly constructed as unimaginative cubes of brick and wood, and were startlingly similar in appearance to many modern urban project houses. When concrete came into general use, they became more solid, but were still dark, overcrowded and unsafe. Fires were common– despite Augustus' fire brigade—and destructive.

The streets between the *insulae* were not much better. Away from the *fora* and the splendid approaches to the emperor's palace and the Senate House, they were narrow and noisy, unlit at night and clogged with traffic by day. The droppings of hundreds of mules, horses and oxen were smelly and attracted insects, especially malaria-carrying mosquitoes from the marshes which, for all their efforts, the Romans never succeeded in draining effectively. And yet for all its dirt and unpleasantness and danger, Rome under Augustus somehow remained an exciting and habitable city: it was after all, as one of his poets said, the capital of the whole world.

The Golden Age of Latin Literature

The last years of the Roman republic and Augustus' principate, like the second half of the fifth century BC in Athens, was one of those brief moments in history where an unusually large number of unusually gifted writers suddenly burst together into notice. There seems to have been, however, no stimulus in common. Most of the great works of Athenian literature were composed in wartime, and it seemed to make no difference whether the Athenians were triumphant or demoralized; some of the most distinguished writers in Latin flourished in times of civil disturbance and uncertainty, and some in the years of stability that followed.

Cicero and Caesar

Cicero probably thought that his life's greatest achievement was his consulship of 63 and his rescue of Rome from the alleged dangers of Catiline's conspiracy; but posterity knows better.

The fact is that Cicero is one of those rare figures more admired for what they said than for what they did. His failure to achieve his political ends has not taken away the gloss of his skills as an orator. He was a lawyer before he became a politician, and the texts of more than fifty of his speeches in the courts and before the Senate have been preserved because—as was the fashion—he wrote them down after their delivery and had them published. His mastery of calm, reasoned argument, of invective, of sly irony, of sarcasm, makes him a model for public speakers even today. Most memorable are the speeches he made in court against Verres, the governor of Sicily, and, in the Senate, his attacks on Catiline in 63 and Mark Antony in 44.

Cicero was also an addicted letter-writer. He wrote to his friends, to his brother Quintus, who was also murdered in the proscriptions of the Second Triumvirate, and to his brother-in-law Atticus. He wrote not only about family matters, but also in minute detail about the events of Roman politics, so that his letters provide both a touching look at his private feelings and an invaluable source for historians of the final years of the republic. During Caesar's dictatorship, when Cicero was not in office, he withdrew from public life for eighteen months: in the privacy of his study he wrote poetry (most of what has survived is pretty bad) and a large number of philosophical essays—partly interpretations of Plato and Aristotle, partly the exposition of his own Stoic beliefs. In contrast to the fury of his speeches, these meditations are soothing and peaceful, and their themes are still worthy of consideration. He pondered, for example, the pleasures and difficulties of *Old Age*, the comfort of *Friendship,* and the moral *Duties* of a citizen.

While Cicero was writing philosophy, Caesar was dashing off *Commentaries* on his two most important campaigns, the Gallic war and the civil war against Pompey. As they stand, the

Commentaries, which he intended to polish into formal histories during his retirement, are no more than drafts: their Latin is usually simple and direct, but the expression is sometimes awkward and occasional sentences are of immense length and complexity. *De Bello Gallico* used to be widely read by students as their first taste of "real Latin." Though it has recently lost its popularity because of its detailed recitals of route marches, battles and skirmishes, it still contains much interesting material on the customs of the Gauls, such as this account of their religious practices:

> *The lives of the Gauls are entirely bound up in their religion, and for this reason those who are threatened by some danger, or who are going off to war, either offer up other men as sacrificial victims or promise themselves to the gods at a later date. And they ask the Druids to take proper charge of the sacrifices, because they think that they can satisfy the gods only if other men's lives are exchanged for their own.*
>
> *The Gauls also hold public sacrifices… Sometimes they will construct a statue of enormous size made of intertwined vines; they then fill the arms and legs with living men, and set the whole thing on fire, so that the men perish in the flames. The immortals, they think, particularly welcome the sacrifice of those who have been caught pilfering, or in any other antisocial behavior. But if there is a shortage of criminals, then they will be satisfied with innocent victims instead.*

(Caesar: *De Bello Gallico* vi.16)

Catullus, Horace and Ovid

Roman poets based their work on Greek models, with regard both to theme and meter. One of the earliest and most passionate of the Greek lyric poets was Sappho, who was imitated closely by Catullus, the most passionate poet of the Romans. Catullus was born in Cisalpine Gaul, where his father was governor during the dictatorship of Sulla. He lived most of his short life in Rome, where he fell in love with Clodia, who was about ten years older then he was and, although she was the widow of a distinguished senator, had a bad reputation—she was suspected of murdering her husband and committing incest with her brother. Catullus' affair with her did not go smoothly; much of his poetry is a desperate plea for her affection, as she alternately spurns him and encourages him. Catullus composes in Greek lyric meters as far as possible, but the force of his feeling prevents them from being mere imitations. In a complimentary reference to Sappho, he always calls Clodia "Lesbia," and indeed one of his most famous poems is a translation into Latin of one of Sappho's:

> *He seems to me to be equal to the gods,*
> *And—if I may say such a thing –*
> *To be actually happier than the gods:*
> *Anyone who, sitting opposite you,*
> *Can look at you over and over again*
> *And hear you gently laughing...*

(Catullus: 51)

Love-sickness does not destroy his sense of humor: he addresses Lesbia's pet sparrow cheerfully as well as enviously, and when it dies he writes a mock funeral ode in its honor:

> *Men of good taste and fine discrimination,*
> *Come join the gods of love in lamentation,*
> *As Lesbia mourns her darling bird's demise –*
> *A bird she valued more than her own eyes.*
> *To him alone she turned attentive ears;*
> *In her alone he placed his hopes and fears.*
> *As children with their mother, so did he*
> *Chirp his affection, hopping on her knee.*
> *Now he's in Hades, whence (you will have learned)*
> *No mortal traveler ever has returned.*
> *You powers of gloom and sin, may you be cursed!*
> *All that is best, you turn into the worst.*

You snatched away that sparrow, now deceased:
By killing beauty, you become the beast.
It's all your fault: because her bird is dead,
My Lesbia's eyes are all puffed up and red.

(Catullus: 3)

But in the end she leaves him angry and miserable:

I hate her: I love her.
Do you understand me?
I certainly don't know what to think myself.
But it's true: and I'm in agony.

(Catullus: 85)

Horace (Quintus Horatius Flaccus) is a somewhat later imitator of the Greek lyric poets. His tone is more careful and controlled than Catullus', and his love poetry has more charm than bite. His main skill is in his ordered use of the language and his ability to make a few words say a very great deal. He is most convincing in his poems about the delights of life in the Italian countryside:

Faunus—lover of the nymphs who flee before you:
Please move gently over my estate
And my sun-warmed fields;
Please, when you go, be kind to all my young things.

At the end of the season,
I will sacrifice a young goat to you.
And I'll make sure that the bowl that Venus loves
Is filled to the brim with wine.
And I'll have my ancient altar smoking with incense...
The farmer who has been digging the earth
Till he hates it
Will be happy now, dancing on it: one—and two—and three.

(Horace: *Odes* iii.18)

Unlike Catullus', Horace's origins were very humble. He was descended from slaves, and his father sold up most of his small farm to send his son to school in Rome, where he studied diligently and began to write. After the murder of Caesar, he served in Brutus' army at the battle of Philippi, but ran away during the fighting. When he returned to Rome, he was taken under Maecenas' wing and quickly switched his support to the new regime:

> *If a man has justice in his heart and is unbending in his purpose, he can never be swayed by the insistence of anyone who urges him to do what is not right... Even if the whole world were to collapse about him, he would still stand unafraid among the ruins.*
>
> *With such unassailable resolve as this, Pollux and the wandering Hercules came after long struggles to the heights of starry Olympus; and there, lying back on his couch with a bright shining face, already drinking nectar among the immortal gods, they find Augustus himself.*

(Horace: Odes iii.3)

It was his unregretted military life which perhaps gave Horace the inspiration for his most famous line, the gallant *dulce et decorum est pro patria mori*. But patriotism is followed by a cooler honesty:

> *To die for your country is a fine and fitting end:*
> *But even deserters find that death is never far away.*
> *So what if a young man has a horror of war,*
> *So what if his knees are knocking, or he turns his back in*
>   *fright?*
> *How would that help him?*

(Horace: Odes iii.2)

The third important lyric poet of this period is Ovid (Publius Ovidius Naso): most of his life was uneventful but he lived well on the income from his writing, which mingled passion, irony, and dry humor with an engaging skill in telling a good story. He was best known in his own time—and still is—for the *Metamorphoses*, a long poem retelling all the Greek myths which involve someone being changed into someone or something else, and finishing with the expectation, like Horace's, that Augustus will be changed into a god. An equally popular work, the *Ars Amatoria*, is a light-hearted instruction manual on seduction as well as a satire on the seamy side of aristocratic life in Rome. Ovid perhaps had some first hand knowledge of this, for he himself became involved with a scandal (possibly connected with the emperor's daughter Julia) and Augustus deported him to Tomi, on the shore of the Black Sea. It was a rough voyage:

Gods of the sea and sky—what is left now except prayer? –
Please don't shake apart the timbers of my poor ship.
Help! How huge are the mountains of water rearing up over us!
You'd think they were about to touch the stars of heaven.
How deep are the valleys carved out by the water receding!
You'd think they were about to touch the depths of hell.
Wherever I look—nothing but sea and sky:
The one swollen with waves, the other angry with clouds.
And between them the gale, howling frightfully,
The seas don't know which master to obey.
At the helm, the steersman hesitates: should he head into the wind,
Or turn away? Among such horrors his seamanship is useless.

(Ovid: *Tristia* i)

Ovid hated his life in exile, but he continued to write poetry; his last book of poems was essentially a plea to be allowed to return to Rome.

Vergil

Born in the country in 70, Vergil (Publius Vergilius Maro) moved to Rome, where he came under the influence of Catullus' circle of friends; he gave up any idea of a life in politics when the civil war broke out in 49. After Caesar's death, Maecenas took him in hand and made sure that, like Horace, he was loyal to the new emperor.

Early in his career, Vergil wrote the *Eclogues*, poems of country life in the style of the Greek writer Theocritus. Then came the *Georgics*, modeled on Hesiod's *Works and Days*, a didactic poem about farming which includes the most detailed surviving story of Orpheus and Eurydice. His major work was an epic poem in the style and meter of Homer called the *Aeneid* (the story of Aeneas). The work was commissioned by Augustus in 26, and was nearly finished at Vergil's death in 19. On his deathbed, Vergil asked that the manuscript should be destroyed, but Augustus pretended not to have got the message.

Aeneas was a Trojan hero who makes a few brief appearances in the *Iliad*, and there was a legend that, after he had escaped from the sack of Troy, he had landed in Italy, and was in fact an ancestor of the founders of Rome. However, Vergil's epic about Aeneas' adventures is only the framework that he uses to set forth a justification of Rome's manifest destiny to rule an "empire without end", in which he ingeniously includes passages in praise of the Roman character, of the Italian landscape, and selected heroes of Roman history.

The format of the first half of the *Aeneid* closely follows that of the *Odyssey*: many of Aeneas' adventures, like Odysseus', are told in a first person narrative; like Odysseus, he encounters the Cyclopes, is rescued from shipwreck, becomes involved in a difficult love affair, and visits the underworld:

> *Between jagged rocks a deep cleft gaped wide open,*
> *leading down to a cave. Black standing water protected*
> *it, black shadows arched over it, black breath seeped*

from it in swirls of poisonous air, so that no birds could safely fly above it...

The world that they entered was sunk in the darkness under the deep earth; if mortals have ever heard of it, it is only by leave of the gods who rule it. It is a formless country of smoldering water and ghosts and shadows and silence stretching endlessly through the night. Can you imagine trying to find your way through an unfamiliar wood after sunset? Can you imagine no light, no shade, no color—just the moon flickering vaguely in a cloud-smeared sky? They traveled alone across the dreary, empty land, and came to the gates of hell...

From here a path led down to a river, seething furiously among deep marshy pools. Mud-bubbles swelled and burst and spat up ooze scoured from the bottom. On the bank a man stood on guard, a daunting and disgusting sight: a filthy cloak was twisted over his shoulders, and a tangled white beard rambled down his chin. He seemed impossibly old, but his eyes glowed with untouched youth, a sure sign that he was in fact a god. He was the master of the rust-gray ferry which carried the dead across the river; he steered it and tended its sails himself. A great crowd pressed down to the edge of the river, as many as the leaves that fall from the trees at the first snap of frost, as many as the birds which, warned by cold weather that it is time to depart for the sunshine of the south, flock together for their stormy migration across the sea. There were mothers and husbands, warriors who had sacrificed their lives in battle, little boys, unmarried girls, young men who had died before their parents—and each one of them begged to be taken across the first, clutching at the surly boatman in their passionate desire to reach the farther side.

(Vergil: *Aeneid* vi. 124 ff.)

The *Iliad* is the model for the second half. Once landed in Italy, Aeneas' forces have to fight a hard campaign against the Latins: Aeneas, like Achilles, has a new shield made for him by Vulcan, on which are depicted famous scenes in future Roman history, including the battle of Actium; and there are vivid accounts of pitched battles and bravery in single combat:

> *Aeneas' spear cut through Mezentius' shield—three layers of bronze and three layers of ox-hide—into his groin. He fell, bleeding badly, and both Aeneas and Lausus ran up to him: Aeneas rejoicing over a wounded enemy, and Lausus weeping miserably for a much-loved father—poor Lausus, whose difficult death and glorious deeds will never be forgotten...*
>
> *As Aeneas came up with his sword raised to deliver the final blow, Lausus jumped between them. The Latins cheered him on, and put up a screen of missiles until such time as Mezentius could crawl away under the cover of Lausus' shield. Aeneas was forced to halt and protect himself. If you can think of a hailstorm or a downpour lashing a valley, as farmworkers run for shelter, and travelers crouch beneath high river-banks or rocky overhangs, waiting for the sun to come out again, you will be able to imagine Aeneas' position...*
>
> *At last Aeneas buried his sword deep in Lausus' body: the point went through his shield and through his breastplate—if only his armor had been as strong as his determination!—and through the tunic which his mother had woven for him with strands of gold. His lungs filled with blood, and his sad spirit left his body, floating away on the breeze to the world below. But when Aeneas saw the strange pallor on his face and knew that he was dying, he remembered his own devotion to Anchises... And he called on his companions to help him lift Lausus' body, and wipe away the blood which had clotted in his hair.*
>
> (Vergil: *Aeneid* x. 782)

Above all, Vergil never forgets that all human life and achievement is, in the end, steeped in sadness: *Sunt lacrimae rerum, et mentem mortalia tangunt* (Everywhere there are tears—what humans do will always touch them in their hearts).

Livy

The Romans were fascinated by their own past and were enthusiastic students of history. The most distinguished historian of Augustus' principate was Livy (Titus Livius), who came to Rome from northern Italy early in the principate, and whose scholarship soon caught the emperor's attention. Livy wrote a history of Rome—in a hundred and forty-two books—from its foundation by Romulus and Remus to his own time. Of this work, the only sections that have survived are those that deal with Rome's early history up to the sack of the city by the Gauls in 390, and with the second Punic war, along with summaries (*Epitomes*) of the rest by ancient commentators. Livy conceived of his history as an epic in prose to stand alongside the *Aeneid*. He therefore paints many of his characters larger than life, and in many incidents he has elaborated the facts in order to make them romantic illustrations of the courage and integrity of the great Romans of the past. As a source, then, Livy's work may be faulted for its lack of historical accuracy and objectivity, but it is still read and praised for its portrayal of history as drama, the unfolding of great events that build to a triumphant climax.

Torso of a general in full armor. (Photograph © 2004 Museum of Fine Arts, Boston)

16. Pax Romana

The Roman Empire after the death of Augustus

Augustus died exhausted (or poisoned by Livia?) in AD 14, at the age of seventy-seven. The Senate at once voted that he should become a god, and then, as he had instructed them, confirmed his stepson Tiberius as the next emperor. The transition was smooth: unlike Alexander the Great's empire, which collapsed soon after his death in 323 BC, the empire that Augustus had founded outlasted him comfortably, despite the varied character and competency of subsequent emperors. Some of Augustus' successors were bad, some mad, and some were administrators of exceptional ability, men of wisdom and generosity. The best of them were always mindful of the welfare of their people, and more often than not they were tolerant of the different religions and cultural traditions that characterized an empire covering nearly all of what they considered to be the whole world. If ever there was resistance and rebellion, it expressed opposition to the policies or whims of individual emperors, never to the institution of the Empire itself. This is not, however, the stuff to inspire exciting historical narrative. Contemporary historians tended to make the most of small-scale military movements, trivial diplomatic incidents and the many scandals within the emperors' immediate circle. Even significant social movements below the surface, such as the rise of Christianity, went largely unheralded and perhaps unnoticed by the Romans themselves.

Tiberius: AD 14 – 37

Tiberius, despite his unhappiness at the manner in which he had been selected as Augustus' heir, began his reign with a period of solid and unspectacular administration. But he could not hide for long the arrogance that had always been typical of his father's family. He scorned the habits of deference that the Senate had learned from Augustus; and he could not hide the fact that the daily duties and ceremonies of his job bored and depressed him.

> *The purpose of history is to promise to record good deeds so that they can be praised, and to threaten to hold up bad words and actions for the disapproval of posterity. But these times were so rife with depravity or ill-intentioned flattery that the leaders of the state had to protect their reputations by currying favor with others; those who had already been consul, along with those who were yet to take up public office, and a great many senators of no importance whatsoever, vied with each other in making inappropriate and toadying proposals. They say that Tiberius, whenever he left the Senate House, used to say: "They are fit to be nothing but slaves." Even he, who saw no value in a free state, grew impatient with the general tolerance of servility.*
>
> (Tacitus: *Annals* iii 65)

When he had been adopted as Augustus' son, Tiberius had been required to bypass his own son Drusus as his heir, and instead to adopt his nephew Germanicus—a cognomen won as a result of successful campaigning in the north. Now, as Tiberius became more moody and aloof, Germanicus became more and more popular, so that when he unexpectedly died in his camp (was he poisoned? was he killed by witchcraft?), gossip in Rome suggested that Tiberius was somehow responsible. Tiberius began to imagine plots against himself, and encouraged informers to report rumors, insults or even jokes against him. He ordered treason trials and executions.

By 26, Tiberius had had enough of Rome. At the suggestion of Sejanus, the commander of the praetorian guard, he withdrew to his villa on Capri, where he is said to have indulged in unmentionable vices and endless self-pity. Sejanus, left in charge in Rome, controlled what the emperor was told or was not told, and appointed his own friends to army commands. But he went too far when he began to ingratiate himself with the Senate and with Tiberius, in the hopes of being appointed the next emperor, and Tiberius had him put to death as a traitor.

Another incident that occurred when Tiberius was on Capri was a disturbance in the new province of Judaea, caused by that same Jesus who had been born during Augustus' census. For some years Jesus had been an itinerant religious teacher, finding most of his support among the poor people of the countryside. Calling himself the son of God or the King of the Jews, he preached to anyone who would listen of the approaching Kingdom of God, which had been foretold by Jewish prophets for many generations. But he was too radical for the traditional Jewish teachers, and the Romans suspected that he was plotting an uprising which would restore the deposed royal family of Judaea, even though he himself was careful not to confuse religious and secular obligations.

> *And the chief priests and the scribes... watched him, and sent forth spies, which should feign themselves just men, that they might take hold of his words, that so they might deliver him into the power and authority of the governor.*
>
> *And they asked him, saying, "Master, we know that thou sayest and teachest rightly, neither acceptest thou the person of any, but teachest the word of God truly: is it lawful for us to give tribute unto Caesar, or no?"*
>
> *But he perceived their craftiness, and said unto them, "Why tempt ye me? Show me a penny. Whose image and superscription hath it?"*
>
> *And they answered and said, "Caesar's."*
>
> *And he said unto them, "Render therefore unto Caesar the things which be Caesar's, and unto God the things which be God's."*

(King James Version: *St. Luke's Gospel* xx.20)

Finally infuriated by the mock-regal style of Jesus' entry into Jerusalem in the spring of 33, a local magistrate named Pontius

Pilate had him tried and crucified—the standard punishment for a non-Roman or a slave found guilty of sedition. In Rome the affair was dismissed as just another example of the unrest that was common in Judaea.

Tiberius spent the last eleven years of his reign as a hermit on Capri *solus et senex* (alone and old), and he died there in 37. However he could not make up his mind whom he should commend to the Senate as his successor. Instead, he left it up to the Senate to make the choice between Germanicus' son Gaius (nicknamed Caligula, for the little army boots that his father's soldiers had made for him when he was a child) and his own grandson Gemellus. The Senate settled on Caligula.

Caligula: AD 37 – 41

The young Caligula, like his predecessor, started his reign well, but he fell ill and, on his recovery, seemed to have gone mad. He was rude to members of the Senate. He spent money lavishly on his private entertainment. He was rumored to have made his horse a consul, and to have given it a marble stall and a purple blanket. More seriously, he took delight in being unexpectedly cruel to friends or total strangers, and he put to death without trial those whom he imagined to be his enemies.

> *His favorite method of execution was to inflict upon his prisoner a series of small wounds which did not affect his vital organs. His order "Make this man aware that he is dying" was often quoted.*
>
> *His favorite line of poetry was Oderint dum metuant (Let them hate me so long as they fear me).*
>
> *He went about complaining that times were bad, particularly because there had been no famous disasters. "No one will remember my reign," he said, "because everyone is so prosperous." He often prayed for a military defeat, or for pestilence, fire or famine—or, failing all else, an earthquake.*

(Suetonius: *Caligula* 30, from *Lives of the Twelve Caesars*)

Unrest grew in Rome, even among the praetorian guard. A few of them, who could no longer tolerate his vices and excesses, decided to act, and they beat him to death in a deserted corridor of his palace.

Claudius: AD 41 – 54

Caligula had of course made no provision for a successor; but the praetorian guardsmen found his uncle, Claudius, hiding behind a curtain during the confusion that followed the assassination. They dragged him out and proclaimed him emperor on the spot. The Senate did not have the nerve to disagree, though Claudius was an unimpressive figure indeed. He stammered, his face twitched, he limped; he seemed almost half-witted. Yet behind his physical deformities (he had perhaps contracted polio as a child) he had a keen mind: he had been a pupil of Livy's and had written a book about Etruscan antiquities.

Now suddenly in the public eye, Claudius made no attempt to disguise his awkwardness. In his new position, he realized, he might have enemies, and it might be an advantage if they did not take him seriously. As it turned out, Claudius was a competent and imaginative administrator. He enlisted freedmen into the civil service and gave them significant responsibilities, especially in financial affairs. He granted Roman citizenship on a generous scale to provincials, and seated a group of Gallic tribal chiefs in the Senate, to which he returned some of its decision-making powers.

Claudius' foreign policy was less conservative than that of Augustus or Tiberius. When he was dissatisfied with the performance of three of the eastern client-kings, he took their kingdoms away from them and turned them into provinces. And to show that he was as good a soldier as his brother Germanicus, he did what Caesar had not been able to achieve, and annexed a fourth new province, Britain, where he maintained order with an impressive show of force. The number of British place-names ending in

—chester or—cester (from *castra*: camp) indicates the size and spread of the Roman military presence there.

To celebrate the conquest of Britain, Claudius gave to his son the *cognomen* of Britannicus. However, the boy was not to become his heir. Claudius' second wife, Agrippina—she was the sister of Caligula, and therefore also his niece—began to push the claims of her son by a previous marriage, Nero. Agrippina was a woman of ferocious determination, and Claudius was quite unable to stand up to her. In 54, he died suddenly after eating some mushrooms (had Agrippina poisoned them?) and the Senate, well satisfied with the events of his reign, voted that, like Augustus, he should become a god. And then, in deference to Agrippina, they voted that Nero was to become the next emperor.

Nero: AD 54 – 68

Like his predecessors, Nero made an excellent first impression, but the pathological insecurity of the Claudian family quickly asserted itself. Nero early began to resent his mother's constant presence. Agrippina appeared beside him at state functions, and had her portrait placed beside his on coins; and on occasion, it was said, she even slept with him. Finally he decided to be rid of her and his young rival, Claudius' son Britannicus. Britannicus was hastily murdered and buried in secret; but Agrippina presented a more difficult problem, for she kept an armed escort with her at all times. On his first attempt on her life, Nero arranged for her to go on a moonlight sail on a yacht that was designed to collapse when it was far out at sea. The yacht fell apart more or less according to plan, but Agrippina was tougher than he had expected, and she managed to swim ashore. The next time Nero was less subtle: he simply hired a gang of thugs who broke into her villa and stabbed her to death.

The government of the Empire, on the other hand, went forward more efficiently. For the most part, the provinces remained content, and Nero's financial and economic management was effective. In order to make easier the operations of Roman merchants, he had the harbor at Ostia dredged, and he dug out the first ceremonial spadeful in an unfortunately unsuccessful attempt to have a canal cut through the Isthmus of Corinth. Only at the end of his reign was there trouble—mutinies among Roman troops in Gaul, and further disturbances in one or two of the other provinces. In Britain, a tribal queen called Boudicca (also known as Boadicea), protesting the cruelty and rapacity of the Romans, led a rebellion which was put down with considerable difficulty. Just before her final defeat, she addressed her army with such courage that even a Roman historian was impressed.

> *"Today I am not a queen defending my kingdom or my possessions; today I am an ordinary woman seeking vengeance.*
> *"The Romans have taken away my freedom. The Romans have beaten me. The Romans have raped my daughters. Their greed has left no one untouched, not even the very old or the very young. But our gods will help us; they have already annihilated the one Roman legion which has dared to face us. The rest of them are holed up in their camps, looking for a way to escape us. The Romans are scared of our war-cries and war-dances even before they have faced us in the field.*
> *"Be ready to win this battle or to die. I am a woman, and that at least is what I intend to do. If any man wants to stay alive, let him—it will only be in order to become a slave."*

(Tacitus: *Annals* xiv.39)

In any case, administration, wars and public works soon took second place in Nero's mind to art and music. He had long fancied himself as a lyre-player and composer, and he now became completely preoccupied with private practice and public performance. He made tours of Italy, Greece and Asia, entering competitions wherever he went—and of course winning all of them. Everywhere he was met with enthusiastic and sometimes genuine applause.

Music seemed a harmless hobby, and in the beginning it kept the emperor out of trouble; in the end, however, it made him forget reality altogether. In 64 a serious fire destroyed much of the city of Rome; but apparently all that Nero did about it was to stand on the roof of his palace watching the blaze and reciting passages from the *Odyssey* about the sack of Troy. And there is no doubt that his behavior after the fire had been put out was equally callous. He showed little sympathy for the people who had lost their homes; and although he announced an extensive plan to rebuild the city, it turned out to be first and foremost a plan to construct ever more luxurious quarters for himself.

Nero had suddenly become unpopular, and unpopularity made him nervous. He therefore tried to distract attention from himself by bringing charges of arson against unspecified members of a new Jewish religious movement that had recently spread to Rome. The movement was named after its founder Jesus (also known as Christ, from the Greek word for "anointed"), who had himself been executed for treason during Tiberius' principate, but whose teachings had become attractive. But Nero's attack on the Christians had nothing to do with their beliefs, for the Romans had always been tolerant of different religions. Throughout their history they had cheerfully mixed other people's religious ideas with their own, and particularly since the time of Augustus Roman soldiers had brought back all sorts of exotic cults from Asia.

But the Christians' constant references to the coming of the Kingdom of God made it easy to accuse them of crimes against the state. Furthermore, they had offended Roman conservatives by including woman and slaves as equals in their community, and by all reports they were cannibals as well: did not their central ritual consist of eating the body of their founder? Their activities in Rome were carried out in secret, and they often hid themselves in underground caves. However, Nero hunted them down and sent them in large numbers into the circus to feed the lions or to be tortured and put to death. Legend says that among the first victims were the apostle Paul, who had first brought Christianity to Rome, and Jesus' disciple Peter, whose cathedral, many years later, would be built on the spot where Nero was supposed to have had him crucified.

The persecution of the Christians and the passing of time made the ordinary Romans forgot their frustration with Nero. But some of the senators vigorously opposed his life of increasing extravagance and his obsession with his lyre. Rumors of plots against him began to circulate, and, as they had under Tiberius, informers appeared to spread the rumors. As Nero became ever more unbalanced, the praetorian guard began to look around for other possible emperors, and the Senate, regaining some of its old republican confidence, finally voted to depose him. In a fit of acute depression, Nero committed suicide. His last words were: "*Qualis artifex pereo* (What an artist the world is losing in me)."

The interior of the Colosseum: raked rows of seats and multiple entrances at different levels resemble the layout of a modern stadium. The floor of the arena (now lost) was covered with sand to soak up any spilled blood; and below the arena were the dressing rooms and cages for the animals. (Art Explosion)

The "Year of the Four Emperors": 68 – 69 AD

Nero was the last emperor to come from Augustus' and Livia's extended family, the last of the so-called Julio-Claudian dynasty. To succeed him, the Senate appointed Galba, who was governor of Spain. Then within a year Galba was followed onto the throne by three other provincial governors—Otho, Vitellius and Vespasian—who in turn disputed the succession and used his army to support his own claim. It was a bewildering year at best; and at worst a dangerous one—for both politicians and generals. Many expected a return to the bad old days of the failing republic, and it was feared that the unusual number of fierce thunderstorms and lightning strikes that year had only gone to prove that the gods were more interested in punishing Rome than in preserving peace. But the inner strength that Augustus had built into his administrative machinery held the Empire together through all the upheavals, until it could be steadied by Vespasian, the last of the "four emperors."

The Flavian Emperors: AD 69 – 96

Vespasian (his full name was Flavius Vespasianus) reigned for ten years (69 – 79), and, determined to allow none of the confusion that had preceded his own accession, he arranged with the Senate that he should be succeeded by his sons Titus (79 – 81) and Domitian (81 – 96). The Flavian emperors were dedicated to the preservation of calm and to improving the imperial finances, which had been greatly diminished by Nero's extravagance and the expenses of the wars of 68/9. Vespasian introduced new taxes and sold off large tracts of the emperor's own estates in Egypt, and added more and more non-Italians to the Senate, so that it now became truly representative of the Empire as a whole.

While provincial administration became generally more efficient, the unrest which routinely simmered in Judaea broke out into open rebellion in 70. The revolt was crushed by the emperor's son Titus: he sacked Jerusalem and destroyed the Temple, though the fortress of Masada held out until 73, in a struggle against long odds that stands in history alongside the Spartan defense of Thermopylae. To celebrate Titus' successes a triumphal arch and the amphitheater known as the Colosseum were built, and the persecution of the Christians, who were not necessarily distinguished from the Jews, continued sporadically for the next quarter century.

At home, there was a natural disaster. In 79, at the beginning of Titus' reign, the volcano of Vesuvius (on the coast just south of Rome) erupted and buried the seaside resorts of Pompeii and Herculaneum under a deep layer of lava and ash. The houses and shops were preserved beneath the debris with many of their artifacts nearly intact: furniture, lamps, jewelry, pots and pans, frescoes and graffiti on the walls, mosaics on the floors—even the food in the cupboards, and meals abandoned on the tables. The two towns remained buried until the seventeenth century, when excavations began which would provide a complete record of daily life in an ordinary, fairly prosperous Roman town of the early Empire. Apparently there had been enough warning for many of the inhabitants to escape; one of the few victims was the famous naturalist Pliny the Elder, who lingered too long in order to find out what a volcanic eruption looked like in close-up. But his nephew, Pliny the Younger, survived and wrote, in a letter, about what he had witnessed:

> *About one o'clock in the afternoon, my mother noticed a cloud of unusual size and shape. She called for her sandals and went up to higher ground from where she could better observe the strange sight. A cloud was rising up over a mountaintop—later on we realized that it was Mount Vesuvius—which resembled a pine-tree more then anything else: it rose up in a long column like a trunk, and then spread out sideways like branches. To my uncle it meant only a phenomenon which had to be examined more closely; he ordered a boat to be got*

ready, and told me that I could come with him if I wanted, but I said I had some work to do—by chance he had just given me some notes to write up. As he left the house, he received a note from Rectina, who was very frightened: her house lay right below the mountain, and there was no way she could get out except by boat. She begged him to rescue her from this terrible danger. So my uncle made plans to take boats across, and himself embarked to bring help not only to Rectina but to many other people as well...

Ash was by now falling on the boat, along with chunks of black pumice and red-hot stones. After a while, my uncle said to the helmsman: "Fortune favors the brave. Take the boat to Pomponianus' place." Pomponianus was at Stabiae [five miles south of Pompeii]; he had loaded all his possessions onto boats, convinced that he would have to take flight if the wind were to change... His courtyard was filling up with ash and pumice, so that if he stayed in the house any longer he would not be able to get out. My uncle... decided to go down to the beach and see if he could get away from there; but the sea was running very high. So he spread out a sail for shelter, and constantly had cold water brought to him to drink.

The flames and the stink of sulfur drove everyone else away, but they merely excited my uncle's curiosity. He was helped to his feet by a couple of slaves, but then collapsed. He could not breathe because of the thick smoke, and in any case he suffered from asthma. The next day, when they found his body, it did not have a mark on it; he looked as though he were asleep rather than dead...

It was now six o'clock in the morning. The house was shaking, and it looked as if it were just about to collapse. It did now seem sensible to leave, and a great many people crowded round us and urged us to hurry;

they were really frightened.

Outside the town we stopped. There was much to wonder at, and much to be afraid of. Our wagons were rolling in all directions, even though we were on completely flat ground. We blocked their wheels with stones, but they would not stay still. The earth trembled, and we saw the sea recede and leave the beach covered with sea-creatures, high and dry on the sand. To the north, spurts of flame flickered in the black cloud, like flashes of lightning, only bigger...

Soon the cloud was hanging down over us even more densely, entirely covering the sea. The ash, which we had not noticed much so far, was now everywhere. I looked back. Behind us was a thick pall of smoke, and it was dark—not the dark of a moonless night, but the dark of a room shuttered up with all the lights out. I could hear women crying, babies whimpering, men shouting; some were calling for their parents, some for their children, some for their wives. Some were bemoaning their own fate, some that of their nearest and dearest. Some in their fear of death prayed for death; many people lifted up their hands to the gods, but a larger number suggested that the gods no longer existed, and that the world was drowning in perpetual night. At last the darkness began to fade, until it looked like a haze of smoke or mist; soon it was full daylight, and the sun shone again.

(Pliny the Younger: *Letters* vi)

The writers of the Flavian period are less concerned than those of Augustus' principate with any need to flatter the emperors. So Suetonius' entertaining *Lives of the Twelve Caesars* (from Julius Caesar to Domitian) are sprinkled with irreverent gossip incapable of proof, while the historian Tacitus is a great deal more somber, critical of Augustus and openly hostile to Tiberius and Nero. His *Annals* are an account of events in Rome during the time of the Julio-Claudian dynasty (with Caligula's and most of

Claudius' reign lost), and his *Histories* deal with the Year of the Four Emperors; he also wrote an ethnographic study of the German tribes who would, many years later, overrun the Empire, and a biography of his father-in-law Agricola, a governor of Britain. Of the same period are the *Satires* of Juvenal, poems lampooning the habits and eccentricities of urban Romans; a definitive study by Justinian, still consulted in law schools, of the principles of Roman law; Josephus' *History of the Jewish War* (i.e. the rebellion of 70); and Pliny the Elder's *Natural History*, which contained "twenty thousand facts" and aimed to be a summary of everything that was known about everything.

Vespasian died in his bed at the age of seventy: he must have been conscious that he had done well enough to be voted into divine status like Augustus and Claudius, for his last words were reputed to have been: "*Vae: puto deus fio* (Oh dear—I'm becoming a god, I think.)." Titus, who was on a tour abroad when he died, was also deified. Domitian was assassinated; he had become obsessed with treason and plots against his life, and had turned cruel and capricious. After his death, his statues were pulled down and all inscriptions bearing his name were erased. Even so, it was a sign of the stability that the Flavians had achieved that the Senate was able to choose as his successor without any pressure from the army. For the first time they selected one of their own number—an elderly lawyer named Nerva.

"The Five Good Emperors": AD 96 – 180

The next five emperors are traditionally called "good" because of the excellence of their characters and their administrations, and each of them had the sense to realize the importance of the problem of the succession. They were not related to each other in any way, but each of them followed the same practice whereby he chose a deserving successor early in his reign, adopted him into his own family according to precedent, and trained him carefully to ensure a smooth transition of power.

This system allowed almost a century of uninterrupted stabil-

ROMAN EMPIRE AT ITS GREATEST EXTENT 138 AD

ity and order, during which the emperors and the Senate worked together in cooperative harmony. More and more inhabitants of the provinces were made citizens (the process became automatic in AD 212). Private philanthropy became common: libraries, schools and universities were founded by individual benefactors in Italy and throughout the provinces, and then partly funded by the state. Scholarship flourished, and perhaps the most important work was Plutarch's *Lives* (biographies, written in Greek, of distinguished Greeks and Romans, and an important historical source).

Many of the great surviving monuments of Roman architecture date from this century: aqueducts in Spain and Gaul, the temple of Olympian Zeus in Athens, and Hadrian's wall built right across the narrowest part of Britain to keep out the marauding Scots. In Rome are Hadrian's villa, the new and improved *insulae* at Ostia, and the Pantheon, a domed temple built by Trajan but fronted by an earlier porch which had been dedicated by

Augustus' colleague Agrippa.

Nerva reigned for only two years (96 – 98), and was followed by Trajan (98 – 117), who had the distinction of being the first emperor born outside Italy. He was born in Spain, and had a Spanish mother. On a celebratory column that still stands, he had carved in relief a series of scenes commemorating his conquest of Dacia (modern Romania), the last province to be added to the Empire. After Trajan came Hadrian (117 – 138), who became extremely popular because he spent much of his time on tours of inspection of the provinces of the Empire, which under him reached its widest extent, covering most of western and southern Europe, Asia Minor, the Middle East and North Africa—an area roughly equal in size to the United States east of the Rockies; and there were trade connections as far as India and China in the east and perhaps the Azores Islands in the west. The exception to the general calm and prosperity was Judaea; after a second revolt in 135, the name of the province was changed to Syria Palestina, and Jerusalem was rebuilt, but no Jews were allowed to enter it. However, the official policy against the Christians was softened by both Trajan and Hadrian, who sent letters to provincial governors instructing them that the Christians were to be left strictly alone as long as they were not involved in political agitation.

The greatest days of the *Pax Romana* came in the reigns of the next two emperors. The eighteenth century English historian Edward Gibbon wrote in his *History of the Decline and Fall of the Roman Empire* that Antoninus Pius (138 – 161) "diffused order and tranquillity over the greatest part of the earth. His reign is marked by the rare advantage of furnishing very few materials for the historian." Finally, Marcus Aurelius (161 – 180) became as famous for his ethical teaching—recorded in his *Meditations*—as for his policies. Perhaps Plato, if he had been alive, might have seen in him the nearest approach that any mortal has made to the ideal of the philosopher-king.

17. Decline and Fall

A cliff may look as if it will stand forever; but centuries of surf beating against it will slowly erode it piece by piece, at a rate invisible to the naked eye. No one alive in the first few decades that followed the reigns of the five good emperors could have known that the Empire was beginning the long slide towards its end. With hindsight, however, it is clear that the first signs of decline were already evident, even though historians have never been agreed on the causes for the Roman Empire's collapse. However, most of them believe that it fell because of a complex combination of moral, economic and military failures, rather than any single cause such as epidemics of smallpox or malaria, or a slow poisoning of the population by lead in the waterpipes.

The first omen of future problems showed itself even in the reign of Marcus Aurelius. The excellence of Marcus Aurelius' character was not matched by his wife's, and it was her influence rather than his that was to be seen in their dissolute and worthless son, Commodus, who had been rashly designated as the next emperor. Under Commodus and his successors, Rome entered a period of intermittent chaos, in which the Senate once more dithered feebly while the army, especially the praetorian guard, selected its own emperors. On one occasion the Empire was put up for auction to the highest bidder, and on another it was awarded to a soldier who had won a wrestling competition. Emperors turned into despots who stripped the Senate of its last scraps of authority; they surrounded themselves more and more with luxurious accommodations and customs copied from the kingdoms of the East, and dropped the title of *Princeps* in favor of *Dominus* (Lord or Master).

With their own extravagance everywhere unconfined, the emperors began to be unable to balance their budgets. The expenses of public services and public works, along with the salaries of the bureaucrats who directed them, drifted out of control, and the economy began to fail. For generations the large numbers of available slaves had made agriculture and construction cheap, and there had been no need for technological innovation to make the work more efficient. But now that foreign conquests were a thing of the past, the supply of slaves began to dry up; and the Romans, who had always distrusted change in any case, found themselves with no new ideas as to how to replace them.

But even if the technology had been there, the land itself was everywhere becoming exhausted. As the fertility of the soil wore out, farms were abandoned and the land reverted to wilderness. Similarly, many mines were now worked out, and raw materials became scarce. A drop in production of all kinds coincided with a drop in the birthrate, which in turn began to have an adverse effect not only on the state's income from taxes, but also on the quality and quantity of recruits who were available for the armies stationed along the frontiers. Native Roman soldiers had over the years been replaced with new generations from the provinces, who largely lacked the traditional Roman discipline and dedication. Military service became unpopular, and even slaves had to be drafted to keep the numbers up. If pressure were to be applied along the frontiers by barbarian tribes, the new Roman army might find itself unable to defend them.

And so it happened. The first border raids by the barbarians came as early as 256, followed by a respite for the next hundred and fifty years. During this time of uneasy peace, in 324, a second capital, for administrative and military convenience, was set up in Asia Minor by the emperor Constantine on the site of the old city of Byzantium, which he renamed Constantinople. The new capital was modeled on Rome, although—because Constantine gave considerable support to Christians—it was marked by its Christian churches rather than temples to the Olympian gods.

In 364 the Empire was finally and formally split into eastern and western halves, each with its own emperor. The eastern half settled down into long centuries of prosperity; eventually known as the Byzantine Empire, with Constantinople as its capital, it lasted into the fifteenth century. The western half, however, came under fierce attack form the barbarians. From Germany, the Vandals swarmed into Gaul, Spain and Africa; Alaric the Goth invaded Italy and in 410 temporarily occupied Rome. Britain was evacuated as a result of pressure from the Scots and the Saxons. Attila the Hun ravaged Gaul and Italy. In 455, the Vandals destroyed Rome and left it in ruins, and twenty years later, in 476, the last Roman emperor was deposed. There was no last gallant defiance, no final resistance, no drumrolls. The world at large took little notice of Rome's fall. The only memorable thing about the last of the Caesars is his name, which by a final irony was Romulus Augustulus.

Mosaic from the province of Africa. A donkey (the favorite animal of Vesta, goddess of the hearth) nurses two lion cubs, in a parody of the tradition about the upbringing of Romulus and Remus. (Photograph © 2004 Museum of Fine Arts, Boston)

18. Exegi Monumentum Aere Perennius…

I have built a monument to last longer than bronze.

(Horace)

The Face in the Mirror

If history were fiction, the story of the Roman Empire would have ended with the reign of Marcus Aurelius. After his death, everything moved towards a sad anticlimax, a dying fall that goes on for much too long. It is preferable, in fact, to look back on Rome as it was in AD 180—a powerful empire at its height, whose citizens, even though they represented many different cultures, traditions and religious beliefs, were apparently as contented and unharried as any subject peoples have ever been. To be fair, however, we must remember that we have very little evidence about what these subject peoples may have thought themselves about their situation. Ancient history in general says little about anyone except the rich and famous.

But history is not fiction, and it must consider and analyze with equal seriousness the worst as well as the best of times in any civilization, especially as the Roman world is often disconcertingly similar to our own. Our triumphs, and our disasters, are theirs. We may be as proud as they were of the achievements of our power and prosperity, and as anxious as they were about the responsibilities that power and prosperity bring. We, like them, are perturbed by the difficulties of preserving a democratic society in a turbulent international climate, by fear of tyranny, by the apparent corruption of public figures, by popular engagement with trivia rather than with matters of moment, and by the conflicting demands of national security and personal freedom. And as history should, Roman history provides us with lessons and warnings that we may regard both with pity and terror, as well as living memorials and a remarkable heritage that we should recognize with gratitude.

Constitution and Law

Many modern democratic constitutions have borrowed ideas from the Roman republic—in particular its essential principle of checks and balances. The framers of the United States constitution were all versed in ancient history and, impressed particularly by the theoretical effectiveness of the Senate as a brake on the misplaced enthusiasm of a popular assembly, they decided that the Romans rather than the Athenians should be their model. Roman law, as codified under the Flavian emperors, is the basis of all European legal systems (except for the English Common Law) and the laws of the United States.

But more importantly, Roman history demonstrates how any constitution can work only when it is doing the job for which it was designed, and how it can fall apart when it fails to adapt to a changing political environment. Any system of government, whether democratic or authoritarian, is liable to founder when those who must make decisions become jealous of their privileges but careless of their responsibilities, or when its policies reflect what is easy or expedient rather than what is truly right and just.

Language

Roman soldiers brought Rome with them wherever they served, and in the western provinces their presence was so pervasive that Latin tended to supplant the native languages, or at least to be fused with them. So over the years Latin changed in different ways in different places, until eventually it became the various "Romance" languages of Western Europe: French, Spanish, Portuguese, Romanian and of course Italian. Latin also became one of several important linguistic strands in English, and much English vocabulary is derived from Latin. Today, Latin phrases are still to be seen on official seals and inscribed on public buildings. They serve as mottoes of political, military and academic institutions—for example: *e pluribus unum, semper fidelis, lux et veritas*. Furthermore, many Latin words and expressions have been borrowed unchanged for the terminology of law (*sub poena, sine die, cui bono?, quid pro quo,* arguments *ad hoc* and *ad hominem*), literary reference (*op. cit., ibid., vide supra* or *infra*), as well as for ordinary conversation (*e.g., i.e., alias, alibi, status quo ante, et cetera*).

Until well into the twentieth century, Latin was the language of the Roman Catholic Church (it is still used in the Vatican) and of college and university ceremonial. Latin was widely taught in colleges and secondary schools in Europe and the United States (and in a few civilized enclaves it still is). It was routinely used in scholarly treatises until late in the eighteenth century: when about 1800 a Cambridge undergraduate submitted an essay on botany written in English, it was rejected because the professor "could not stomach the notion of degrading such a science by treating of it in a modern language." And Latin is still used in taxonomy, where a new Latin formulation comes into existence whenever a new species is discovered. Even though for computation the Arabic numerals that came by way of Constantinople supplanted them, Roman numerals are still used to mark clockfaces, dates and chapter headings in books, as well as to distinguish monarchs, popes, children of the same name as their fathers, and American football championships.

Literature

Even after Rome was gone, its literature was saved. Though it was filled with references to pagan gods and rituals, it was faithfully preserved by Christian monks in Europe and Muslim scholars in Byzantium. All through the Middle Ages, Roman manuscripts were copied, annotated and studied, until, during the Renaissance, they were once more published and at the same time began to be translated into English. For instance, Shakespeare, who had "small Latin and less Greek," used North's translation of

Plutarch's *Lives* as the source for his three "Roman plays" (*Coriolanus, Julius Caesar, Antony and Cleopatra*) and borrowed extensively from Golding's version of Ovid's *Metamorphoses*.

Plots and themes from Roman history, legend and mythology, and references to them, appear throughout western literature and, along with a Latinate style, are one of its common denominators and pervasive influences. Until recently, most western speakers and writers were familiar with Latin literature and, having read the original works in school or for their own amusement, could and did quote from them confidently. A story is told of William Gladstone, a British Prime Minister of Queen Victoria's reign, who once stumbled in the middle of a passage from Horace

Eighteenth century etching by Piranesi: "View of the Cow Field." This unromantic name was given to the abandoned Forum in the Middle Ages, and it stuck until the Renaissance. The Corinthian columns on the right belong to the temple of Castor and Pollux. In the background, left center, is the Colosseum. (Photograph © 2004 Museum of Fine Arts, Boston)

during a speech in the House of Commons; the whole House is said to have risen without hesitation and finished the quotation for him.

Art and Architecture

The Romans everywhere adopted Greek styles in public art, and then elaborated upon them with their own modifications. Roman architecture and architectural decoration (mosaics, frescoes, statues, portrait sculpture, carved *cornucopiae*) were a major stimulus for city-planners and designers all over the world both during the days of the Empire and into more recent times. There are copies of Roman ceremonial arches in Paris, London and New York; it is easy to spot the Roman influence in the domed cathedrals of the Virgin in St Petersburg, of Sacré Coeur in Paris, of St Paul in London; in the United States a Roman senator might still feel quite at home in the Capitol and its surrounding monuments, or in Thomas Jefferson's Monticello, or in any of the colonnaded or domed edifices of the "Classical Revival" of the early nineteenth century.

The Transmission of Greek Culture

From the third century BC, but especially after Greece had been taken under Roman protection and then into the Empire, it was the Romans who kept the Greek gods and myths alive, who absorbed Greek ideas, who gathered Greek art and artifacts into their private collections and then flooded the Empire, east and west, with copies.

In particular, the Romans brought Greek literature to Italy and made it the centerpiece of their own literary experience and of their educational system. Greek authors were read, imitated and used as a source of inspiration for Roman poets, historians and philosophers. Greek manuscripts were collected and studied in Roman libraries, and later they were kept safe from the barbarians in the medieval monasteries or in the universities of the

Byzantine Empire. The copies which the monks made were then republished, in the fifteenth and sixteenth centuries, to become the primary stimulus for the Renaissance. Much of what the modern world knows of the Greeks, and much of what it owes to the Greeks, is the gift of the Romans.

Christianity

It is hard to imagine that Christianity would ever have emerged as a world religion without the Romans. Christianity began in a Roman province, and from there spread throughout the Mediterranean and Middle Eastern world along Roman roads and in Roman ships. Its first missionary, Paul, was a Roman citizen who traveled widely, preaching the gospel and writing letters to the Christian communities in the cities of the Empire. His experiences, recounted in the *Acts* and his various *Epistles* in the New Testament, were written in Greek so that they would be understood in the eastern provinces.

For nearly three hundred years Christianity made steady progress even though Christians suffered at various times and for various reasons from official persecution. But under Trajan and Hadrian the persecution stopped. In 324 Constantine presided over the Council of Nicaea, a summit conference of Christian leaders from which emerged the wording of the Nicene Creed, the first formal statement of Christian dogma. Twelve years later, in the Edict of Milan, Constantine granted Christians everywhere in the Empire the freedom to worship as they wished, and instituted Sunday as a day off from work for everyone. The final acceptance of Christianity as the official religion of the Empire was marked in 391 by the shutting down of the oracle at Delphi.

The early church used the Empire as a model for its administration—the Pope was emperor, his bishops were proconsuls, and their dioceses were provinces. As some of Christianity's original Jewish tenets were dropped, it gradually absorbed from Rome and Constantinople some of the ethical teachings of Plato and the Stoic philosophers. About 330, the Bible was published for the first time in an authorized Latin version called the *Vulgate* (the Old Testament was translated from the Hebrew and the New Testament from the Greek), and Latin was adopted in the west as the language of church liturgy.

From the eastern imperial capital of Constantinople, and its Cathedral of St Sophia, emerged the Eastern Orthodox Church, which was compelled to reestablish itself in Greece and in Russia after the Muslims captured Constantinople in 1453. In the west, the Roman Catholic Church survived the barbarian invasions and eventually established itself throughout Europe.

The Church's proselytizing energy, for good or ill, has helped to shape much of the political, diplomatic and cultural history of the west, from the Middle Ages and the Crusades to the Renaissance and the Reformation, and even to the secular activity of evangelical Christians in our own century. The persecution of Christians has led to migrations and the establishment of new nations. Christian missionaries have disseminated far more than scripture through the world, and Christian principles have underlain intellectual questions which, at various moments in history, have affected the thinking and values of millions of people, whether they are Christians or not: the divine right of kings, for example, or the role of women in society, or the separation of church and state, or the religious and ethical implications of scientific discovery. These questions, whose answers continue to shape the modern world, might never have been asked at all if the Romans had not first tolerated Christianity and then encouraged its survival. The Judeo-Christian and the Greco-Roman traditions are still entwined and still remain powerful forces, standing their ground even today on the seven hills of the Eternal City.

Chronological Table of Main Events of Roman History

(Note how events of early Roman history coincide with events in Greece, which are in italics)

1180 BC (trad.)	Fall of Troy: start of Aeneas' legendary journey to Italy
1000 BC (approx.)	*Dorians arrive in Greece.* Latins arrive in Italy?
776 BC (trad.)	*First Olympic Games*
753 BC	Founding of Rome by Romulus and Remus
509 BC	Expulsion of the kings: establishment of Roman republic
506 BC	*Constitution of Cleisthenes in Athens*
494 BC	Creation of office of Tribune of the Plebs
490 – 479 BC	*Persian Wars*
404 BC	*End of Peloponnesian War*
396 BC	Fall of Veii: end of Etruscan wars
390 BC	Gauls occupy Rome
323 BC	*Death of Alexander the Great*
287 BC	Lex Hortensia: decisions of plebeian assembly have force of law
279 BC	Pyrrhus' "victories" in Southern Italy
264 – 241 BC	First Punic War
218 – 201 BC	Second Punic War
146 BC	Sack of Corinth. Third Punic War: the destruction of Carthage
133 – 123 BC	Tribunates of the Gracchi
107 BC ff.	Marius' army reforms
90 BC	Italian (Social) War
82 – 79 BC	Dictatorship of Sulla
72 BC	Spartacus' slave revolt
59 BC	First Triumvirate (Pompey, Caesar and Crassus)

58 – 50 BC	Caesar's conquest of Gaul
49 – 46 BC	Civil war: Pompey v. Caesar
46 – 44 BC	Dictatorship of Caesar
44 BC	Assassination of Caesar
43 BC	Second Triumvirate (Octavian, Antony and Lepidus)
31 BC	Battle of Actium: establishment of Roman Empire
27 BC	Octavian is granted cognomen of Augustus
14 AD	Death of Augustus
33 AD	Crucifixion of Jesus in Judaea
68 AD	The "Year of the Four Emperors"
96 – 180 AD	The "Five Good Emperors"
256 AD	First barbarian raids on Roman borders
312 AD	Edict of Milan: Christianity becomes official religion of the Empire
330 AD	Capital of the Empire moved to Constantinople
364 AD	Empire divided into Eastern and Western halves
455 AD	Rome destroyed by the Vandals
476 AD	Deposition of the last Roman emperor

A NOTE ON SOURCES

Nearly all of the major primary sources for Roman civilization are quoted or mentioned in this book (see index). For more details on these and other sources, students should refer to the relevant entries in the *Cambridge Ancient History,* the *Oxford Classical Dictionary,* or the bibliographies of modern histories. The writers listed below wrote in Latin unless otherwise indicated; some translations are easier to find than others, but all can be found in the Loeb Library series (Harvand University Press) and many of them are included in the Penquin Classics series.

Early Roman History—to the Punic Wars

> Livy: *History*
> Plutarch (Greek): *Lives*

The Punic Wars and events up to 133 B.C.

> Cato: *On Agriculture*
> Livy: *History*
> Lucretius: *De Rerum Natura* (The Nature of the Universe)
> Plautus: comedies
> Plutarch: (Greek): *Lives*
> Terence: comedies
>
> also Polybius (Greek, 2nd century B.C.): *Histories*

The Roman Revolution, 133–31 B.C.

> Caesar: *Gallic War, Civil War*
> Catullus: *Poems*
> Cicero: political and forensic speeches, essays and letters
> Plutarch: (Greek): *Lives*
> Suetonius: *Lives of the Twelve Caesars*
>
> also Sallust (1st century B.C.): *War with Jugurtha, Catiline's Conspiracy*

The Principate of Augustus, 27 B.C.–14 A.D.

Augustus: *Res Gestae*
Horace: *Odes, Epistles, Satires*
Ovid: *Metamorphoses, etc.*
Suetonius: *Lives of the Twelve Caesars*
Tacitus: *Annals*
Vergil: *Eclogues, Georgics, Aeneid*

also Vitruvius (early 1st century A.D.): *On Architecture*

The Julio-Claudian Emperors, A.D. 14–68

Bible, New Testament: *Gospels, Acts, Epistles*
Suetonius: *Lives of the Twelve Caesars*
Tacitus: *Annals*

The Later Emperors, A.D. 68–180

Marcus Aurelius: *Meditations*
Gaius: *Institutes*
Josephus (Aramaic, translated into Greek): *The Jewish War*
Juvenal: *Satires*
Pliny the Elder: *Natural History*
Pliny the Younger: *Letters*
Suetonius: *Lives of the Twelve Caesars*
Tacitus: *Histories, Agricola, Germania*

also Apicius (4th century A.D.): a collection of recipes
      Apuleius (2nd century A.D.): *The Golden Ass* (a novel)

INDEX

Scipio